KINGSTON-UPON

Images of a Rich Transpo

Road - rail -water

by Neville Stead

With photographic contributions from Associated British Ports, Robert Anderson, David Benson, Harry Cartlidge, Stephen Chapman, Malcolm Fussey, Tom Greaves, David Leckonby, Peter Rose, H. B. Priestley, Michael Thompson, and Ray Woodmore

Published by
BELLCODE BOOKS
CHURCH VIEW, MIDDLE STREET.
RUDSTON, EAST YORKSHIRE YO25 4UF
email: bellcode4books@yahoo.co.uk

ABOVE: Until the Beeching axe fell on the Hornsea and Withernsea branch lines in 1964, Hull had several what might be termed inner suburban stations in the east of the city. The first to be encountered on the way out of Paragon station was Botanic Gardens (originally named Cemetery Gates,) this view of which was captured from the signal box. It is clearly the summer holiday season as the diesel multiple unit bound for Hornsea consists of eight cars to cope with all the seaside daytrippers. The Hornsea and Withernsea trains ran a fairly frequent service and were very well used in the summer but that did not save them from the dreaded axe.

A short steam-hauled goods train hauled by an Ivatt 2-6-0 waits in the platform for the signal to clear after the Hornsea train has passed, allowing it to proceed along the direct line to Anlaby Road Junction and on to the marshalling yards west of the city. Meanwhile, a long queue of traffic upper left waits for the crossing gates to open. There will also be queues right and lower left and with this scenario occurring many times a day here and at other similar spots in the city, the level crossings were a source of long delays and great frustration to all road users.

Copyright © 2016 Bellcode Books
ISBN 978-1871233-30-8

Edited by Steve Chapman

Printed in the UK by the Amadeus Press, Ltd., Cleckheaton, West Yorkshire.

INFLUENTIAL EXPERIENCES

I spent my early years at Willerby, down Carr Lane. During the war my mother moved around a bit and for a time she was companion housekeeper to a Mrs. Williamson who had a draper's shop on Main Street - the terrace is still there but the shop isn't. A path went behind the back yards and off this were Anderson shelters. We went in one when there was an air raid. It didn't have a door, just a cloth across the opening because if anything landed nearby a door would splinter everywhere. One night somebody pulled the cloth back and I looked up at the back windows of the terraced houses. All I could see was an orange glow, like sunrise. It was Hull on fire. That was the night of 7th/8th May 1941.

In 1944, just before Christmas, we had a V1 rocket - a "doodlebug" - come down nearby. They usually launched them from mainland Europe but they could reach no further than London, so the Germans had this idea of hanging them underneath a Heinkel 111 and launching them from the North Sea so that they would reach Manchester. But they went everywhere and one dropped into a field just by Springhead water works, about a mile from Carr Lane. It exploded with a big bang and about 600 house were damaged.

Anyway, so much for the war. It will come up from time to time later because it had such an affect on everything this book is about.

I suppose my first direct experience of Hull transport came in 1947 when I started at Hymers College, near Botanic Gardens. I had to catch the bus every morning from Willerby Square. We had a wonderful session because five or six buses turned up - nobody had cars then. They were all ancient petrol-driven single deckers. We didn't care if they broke down - we were only going to school.

The trams had all gone by the time I first got into town but the trolley buses that seemed to glide by, the Corporation buses of many different kinds, and the East Yorkshire buses with oddly shaped roofs, all of them in various blue liveries, could be absorbed in a single eyeful. And there were ships berthed right up to the main shopping streets with railway wagons shunted alongside. Watching North Bridge lift to let a barge or small ship pass along the River Hull was a treat in itself for any young lad.

The trolley buses were wonderful things. You could get speed up quickly and you were away. In school days I scorned the notorious school dinners and went instead to Troxler & Stanley's, a little restaurant on Ferensway. From my table I could look straight out of the window onto the trolley bus wires outside. Sometimes one would come round the corner, off Carr Lane onto Ferensway, and one of the arms would drop off the wires. The thing would stop dead which was quite a laugh to see. A bloke would then appear

East Yorkshire Motor Services 30ft "New Look" AEC Regent No. 651 at Kingston Road, Willerby Square, in November 1957. In the background, the Hull Savings Bank proudly overlooks the square in a time when Willerby was still a village. The draper's shop where the author lived for a time as a child is in the left background.

with a pole and poke it back on again.

At the time, Hull Corporation had mostly AEC buses with fluid flywheel pre-selector gears but during the war they'd been dealt four Leyland TD7s. These had crash gears and it was a real pantomime because the drivers hadn't a clue how to handle them. They'd crunch the gears like there was no tomorrow. It was wonderful stuff. In later years I travelled daily to work on these things.

Clattering over the many level crossings on the buses was a memorable experience. Beyond some of the old crossing gates there would be a station. We'd often be held up in a queue of traffic so it was a case of straining your neck get a view of the train as it passed.

There was a walk from Holderness Road to Hedon Road along Craven Street which followed the Hull & Barnsley railway up on arches and embankments on your left. Eventually you came to a bridge overlooking, towards the city, a vista of railway. Sidings everywhere held wagons loaded with timber; sidings went into a large sawmill on the left and there were lines going to Drypool. In the midst of all this, dwarfed by the scale of scene, was the island platform of Southcoates station, the far end of which had already been seen from the level crossing on Holderness Road. Sometimes I'd carry on along Hedon Road and on

the right were sidings where trains would come in and pilots would take over.

Nearby Southcoates Lane produced another vista. Looking away from the city were stacks of timber and timber stacking sheds, and the lines to Withernsea and King George Dock. Down below on the right were the wonderfully named Sweet Dews sidings. Looking straight ahead from the brow of the bridge, you'd see not only the funnels and derricks of ships at Alexandra Dock, but also the locomotives that shunted the dockside railways. An even better view could be had from the top deck of a bus as it came over the bridge.

Walking by Humber Dock we could see the packet ships that sailed to and from the Continent loading and unloading their passengers and cargo. These old steamers looked so huge to me then but I can't help wondering how many of them would fit into one of the gigantic ships that sail from King George Dock nowadays.

Of course the experience of Hull would not be complete without the paddle steamers. I loved going on the ferries because they used to thump across the water and if you were up top above the wheels you got sprayed. It was short but exciting because when you got across to the other side it was a whole different world - like arriving in another country.

I left Hull many years ago but the inspirational sights I witnessed there have stuck with me and shaped my life since.

In the early years of electric trams, a pair of Spring Bank four-wheelers form a very overcrowded special. The headboard reads: "Olive Branch Lodge Juvenile Tree Gardeners." The date is 18th August 1906.
From an old postcard courtesy R. Woodmore

Introduced in 1873 by the Hull Street Tramways Company, the city's first trams were horse-drawn. Later that century the wonderfully titled Drypool and Marfleet Steam Tramway Co. started a steam tram service on the Hedon Road route. The tramways were taken over by the Corporation in 1898/9, electrified and the various routes converted to double track. The system steadily expanded until reaching its maximum in 1927 with over 20 route miles, 180 trams and, until 1931, its own power station.

The network followed the five main roads radiating from the city centre: to Pickering Park (Hessle Road,) Anlaby Common, Newington, Hedon Road (Marfleet) and Corporation Pier, Ings Road (Holderness Road,) Beverley Road via Newland, and Cottingham Road via Spring Bank.

From 1937 the system was progressively converted to electric trolley bus operation until the last tram ran in June 1945.

ABOVE: No less than four trams are visible in this 1920s postcard view of King Edward Street. No identification for the leading tram is given and the number is largely indiscernible but appears to be in the 170s. If so, it is one of a batch built by Brush of Loughborough in 1915 with Brill bodywork.

BELOW: Tram No. 128, seen here in Prospect Street, was one of 14 built in the Corporation's own workshops in 1909/10 with Mountain & Gibson bodywork. Originally open topped, they were all fully enclosed between 1920 and 1931. *Picture by H B Priestley*

ABOVE: This tram appears to be No. 172. This 1915 series were built with canopies covering the top deck as seen here but most, though not 172, were fully enclosed as per the tram in the previous picture, between 1921 and 1935. On the right is the Yorkshire Penny Bank. *Picture by H B Priestley*

BELOW: This 1935 scene shows tram No. 115 approaching the Haworth Arms public house at the junction of Beverley Road(ahead) and Cottingham Road(left) while on service BC to Cottingham Road. No. 115 was built in 1903 by G. F. Milnes & Co. of Hadley, Shropshire, with Brill bodywork.

ABOVE: Crossley TDD4 trolley bus No. 35 turns back at Anlaby High Road roundabout marking the terminus of service 69. Built 1937 with Cravens bodywork, Metropolitan Vickers 85hp motors and regenerative control, it was scrapped in 1962. When the trolley buses were introduced in 1937 they utilized the former tram routes, apart from those to Hedon Road and Corporation Pier where the trams were replaced by motor buses.

BELOW: Sunbeam trolley bus No. 89, with bodywork by Charles Roe of Leeds, emerging from the depot alongside Newington level crossing on Anlaby Road. No. 89 was one of six built in 1947 with Metropolitan Vickers 95hp motors and rheostatic control. They were the first in a fleet of the new style 8ft wide vehicles. No. 89 was scrapped in 1963.

ABOVE: Trolley bus No. 91 coming under the Hull & Barnsley Railway on Newland Avenue in November 1963. No. 91 was one of ten built in 1948 by Sunbeam with Roe bodywork, Metropolitan Vickers 95hp motors and rheostatic control. It was withdrawn in 1963 and disposed of for scrap in February 1964.

BELOW: Trolley bus No. 84 at Newland Avenue terminus with service 62. Delivered new from Sunbeam with Roe bodywork in 1946, No. 84 was equipped with Metropolitan Vickers 85hp motors and rheostatic control. It was withdrawn in 1963.

ABOVE: North Bridge is one of the iconic moveable bridges which make an impressive sight when lifting for shipping to pass along the River Hull. It was built in 1931 as a Scherzer rolling lift bridge to replace a narrower swing bridge. This view in September 1962 shows trolley bus No. 66 leaving the city with a No. 64 Holderness Road service. Clearly visible on the left is one of the curved ends of the bridge superstructure which rolls downwards as the bridge lifts.

BELOW: Trolley bus No. 23 comes under the former Hull & Barnsley Railway "High Level line" on Chanterlands Avenue while heading for the city centre in June 1954. No. 23 is one of Hull's first trolley buses, one of 26 built by Leyland with Weymann bodywork and Metropolitan Vickers motors in 1937. It was withdrawn for scrap in 1955

ABOVE: Hull Corporation AEC Regent 111 No. 278 passes trolley bus No. 53 at Ings Road terminus, Holderness High Road, in June 1958. A Leyland type TB7 with East Lancs. bodywork, No. 53 was built in 1940 and withdrawn in 1959, after which it was stripped for spares and cut up by the Corporation.

BELOW: AEC Reliance No. 158 overtakes Crossley TDD4 trolley bus No. 40 on Chanterlands Avenue in June 1959. No. 40 was built in 1938 and withdrawn for scrap in 1962. Built in 1957, No. 158 was renumbered 58 in 1967 and withdrawn in 1976.

RIGHT: A moment of inconvenience for some but no doubt amusement for others was when a current collection trolley came off the wires and a long pole was needed to put it back on. On Chanterlands Avenue in January 1962 the long pole is used on No. 71 in this wintry scene.

A problem with the trolley buses of course was that, like the trams before them, they could not just turn round anywhere. There had to be a return loop or a circular route.

BELOW: Trolley bus No. 108 was caught in King Edward Street with a No. 63 Beverley Road service in November 1963. It was on this route that Hull's last trolley bus ran on 31st October 1964, following a withdrawal process begun in 1961, just as concerns were about to be voiced about the damage to health of diesel and petrol fumes in cities, recently proven to be even worse than originally thought. Behind No. 108 are neo-Georgian buildings containing shops and offices erected as part of the city's post-war rebuilding. Such was the wartime devastation of Hull that post-war architects virtually had a blank canvass to work on but Sir Patrick Abercrombie's truly imaginative grand plan to totally rebuild Hull, including its railways, was just too ambitious at a time of great austerity. *Peter Rose*

THE STORY OF MOTOR BUSES IN HULL goes back to 1909 when the Corporation acquired ten vehicles from the Mersey Railway with which it ran a short-lived service between New Cleveland Street and Stoneferry Green. A new start was made in 1921 and over subsequent years the Corporation steadily expanded its network, sometimes acquiring other smaller operators.

Since the 1920s two principal operators have run Hull's bus services - the Corporation and East Yorkshire Motor Services and it remains so today except that Stagecoach at the time of writing run the city buses on behalf of the city council. The Corporation buses carried a blue and white livery whereas East Yorkshire were in one of the most stylish liveries of any bus company: indigo and primrose with the company name in gold Roman capitals. Its coaches were in an equally attractive primrose and mid-blue. East Yorkshire also steadily expanded by acquiring other companies.

Forty five of the Corporation's buses were destroyed in the 1941 blitz and services were only maintained by shipping in replacements from other cities around the country. East Yorkshire's buses were saved from the worst ravages of the bombing by drivers taking them home at night.

Systems were devised whereby the two operators' services were co-ordinated and revenues shared. Corporation buses ran those services within the city boundary whereas East Yorkshire also ran - and still does - services throughout the East Riding and beyond to such destinations as Scarborough and York. On summer Saturdays it once ran to Newcastle using luxury coaches. Another major operator once reaching Hull with services from Leeds was the West Yorkshire Road Car. Co., its buses in a red and cream livery.

Between 1969 and 1987 EYMS was part of the state-controlled National Bus Company and had a standard poppy red and cream livery forced upon it. In 1995 a new livery of burgundy and cream was adopted but a few buses carry varying liveries, including classic indigo and primrose while primrose and mid-blue remains in use for hire coaches. In 2016 EYMS was Britain's biggest independent operator, with a great awareness of its heritage.

Daimler COG5 No. 16 built in 1937 with Weymann bodywork seen posed in 1939. The lettering and livery, complete with city coat of arms below the window line, are worthy of note. This bus was a regular on Service 27, often referred to as the "Fish Dock Doubles." It was withdrawn in 1949.

ABOVE: Some of Hull's earliest double deckers. These early 1930s Leyland TD2 "Titans" are thought to be in the depot yard at Holderness Road awaiting their final journey to the scrapyard. From left they are Nos. 100, 123, 117, 93, 96, and 118. They had all been disposed of by 1949.

BELOW: Guy Arab No. 232 heads a line of Corporation buses on rugby specials for a Hull Kingston Rovers match at Holderness Road in June 1954. Notice the parked push bikes on the left. The Guy Arabs were built between 1943 and 1945 to wartime specifications. No. 232 was one of several rebuilt post-war with 1939 Massey bodywork from withdrawn AECs.

ABOVE: AEC Regent 111 No. 268 crosses the old Drypool Bridge while coming out of the city with Service 41 to Newbridge Road in September 1956. Going upriver from Drypool, other moveable bridges are North Bridge, Jenning Street, Chapman Street(a single span swing bridge,) Stoneferry(nowadays comprising two adjacent dual carriageway spans raised by Dutch-style cantilever arms,) and Sutton Road. Besides these are the railway bridges - Wilmington swing bridge(now carrying only a footpath,) and Sculcoates swing bridge carrying the former Hull & Barnsley line to King George Dock.

BELOW: Guy Arab No. 238 on Beverley Road with the No. 22 Ellerburn Avenue service, also in September 1956 but on a much better day than that above. The policeman directing traffic is another extinct species, except when traffic lights fail.

ABOVE: The view along Jameson Street towards Paragon station on Saturday 18th May 1957. Outside the great Hammonds department store, AEC Regent No. 198 is augmenting trolley buses to East Park on the occasion of a visit to the city by Queen Elizabeth 11 and the Duke of Edinburgh. Whilst the name of Hammonds is now a fond memory, the store is still in business as House of Fraser.

BELOW: AEC Regent 111 No. 335 at Jenning Street bridge, Wincolmlee, whilst diverted due to the royal tour of 18th May1957. Additional interest in the picture is provided by the classic road sign on the left, the coal barge passing underneath the bridge, below right, and, on the far right, the rail-mounted steam grab working at the coal wharf. Similar coal wharves were to be found in York and Leeds, the two steam grabs at Leeds remaining in use well into the 1970s. Jenning Street bridge consists of two lifting spans but nowadays the road is closed and the bridge permanently raised.

ABOVE: AEC Reliance No. 162 negotiates Botanic Gardens level crossing with a No. 15 service to Bricknell Avenue via Chanterlands Avenue in September 1957. Renumbered 62 in 1967, this vehicle remained in service until 1975. Notices on the front and side direct boarding passengers to the front door in order to pay their fare to the driver, the rear door being exit only. It can also be seen that the branding has changed to "Kingston-upon-Hull Corporation Transport."

BELOW: AEC Reliance No. 163 and AEC Regent No. 334 at Wold Road terminus in October 1957. As can be seen, 163 is forming an additional service to Hull Fair, one of the country's biggest and most famous itinerant fairs, held each October on a site next to Walton Street. No. 163 was new in October 1957 when it was the last of nine to be delivered that year. It was renumbered 63 in 1967 and retired in 1973. No. 334 entered service in 1950, ending its days in 1969. Both had Weymann bodywork.

ABOVE: Guy Arab No. 236 was returning empty to the garage when caught on Cottingham Road near the junction with Clough Road in November 1957. Notice the very angular body profile with no stylish curves. This was due to the shortage of skilled coachbuilders and cost during wartime when these buses were built.

BELOW: Guy Arabs Nos. 210, 204, 232, 236, 206, 237, 209 and 216 in Lombard St. bus park in May 1958. The difference in body styles between originals and rebuilt versions are clearly visible.

LEFT: Cottingham Road garage in May 1958 with AEC Regents Nos. 246, 250 and 245 alongside trolley buses. Rails can be seen still set in the floor of this former tram depot.

BELOW: Bricknell Avenue, terminus for North Hull Estate, in May 1958 with AEC Regent 111 No. 280.

ABOVE: Holderness Road garage in June 1958. Fronting the lines of Corporation buses are rebuilt Guy Arab No. 219(left) and AEC Regent 111s Nos. 259(centre) and 307. No. 259 is an earlier 7ft 6 in wide vehicle while 307 is a later 8ft wide version. The garage's past as a tram shed is evident by the old tram lines in the floor.

BELOW: Over time, a number of manufacturers have loaned demonstrators of new models, doubtless with the hope of winning orders. This one, seen at the Willerby Road terminus in July 1958, is AEC Bridgemaster registration No. 76 MME. As its name suggests, it was designed to negotiate low bridges. Compare the width of this bus with those on the previous pages.

ABOVE: AEC Regent 111 No. 272 at the original narrow Drypool Bridge in October 1958 while coming into the city with Service 45.

BELOW: This view on Monday 1st June 1959 shows AEC Regent 111 No. 334 on service No. 58 to Holderness Road, having just crossed North Bridge on its way out of the city. Maintenance of some sort is under way on the right using the Corporation's tower wagon. Also on the right is the National & Provincial Bank while the King's Arms pub is on the left.

ABOVE: Even a double decker bus like AEC Regent No. 263 is dwarfed by the monument to William Wilberforce. No. 263 is crossing the site of Queen's Dock while proceeding along Wilberforce Drive with service 41 in May 1959.

RIGHT: Sutton Road bridge is another River Hull lifting bridge, of similar design to North Bridge but without the concrete facade. Although situated well up-river on the northern outskirts, it was still necessary because the river was navigable to Beverley where until the 1970s there was a shipyard which built many of Hull's trawlers, while at one time barges even went as far as Driffield. It is June 1959 and AEC Reliance No. 165 is on the No. 19 via Beverley Road.

ABOVE: Lowgate as it was in May 1959, affording a striking view of the Wilberforce monument as AEC Regent No. 259 comes along with with service 41.

BELOW: At Priory Roundabout, Spring Bank West, in August 1959 with AEC Regent 111 No. 337. The destination blind states service No. 1 via Chanterlands Avenue. Built in 1953, No. 337 was retired in 1971 and subsequently preserved.

ABOVE: The drive to cut costs by removing conductors and making services driver-only spawned a new breed of rear-engined buses with entrances only at the front. Among those new designs to emerge was the Leyland PDR1 "Atlantean" and demonstrator reg. 398 JTB came to Hull in 1959. It is seen by the Cecil cinema, Ferensway, that September.

BELOW: The Corporation were clearly impressed by the demonstrator as they bought more than 40 Atlanteans between 1960 and 1964 with further batches of later versions into the 1970s. No. 365 had just entered service when photographed crossing the Hessle Road-Cottingham South railway at Newington Level Crossing, Anlaby Road, in February 1962. It was renumbered 165 in 1973, withdrawn in 1978 and scrapped, but some of its sisters saw further service with the West Midlands Passenger Transport Executive.

ABOVE: This busy scene on Beverley Road shows brand new Leyland Atlantean No. 344 approaching Stepney level crossing on Saturday 4th June 1960. There was also a station here served by Hornsea and Withernsea trains and this view is from the footbridge.

LEFT: Atlantean No. 346, one of the first five delivered to Hull in 1960 with 1961 sister No. 349 at Dairycoates terminus on 22nd April 1961. It was to Dairycoates that the last tram ran in 1945.

In the distance is the bridge carrying the former Hull & Barnsley Railway goods line from Springhead to Neptune Street goods yard.

RIGHT: AEC Regent 111 No. 279 stands outside Corporation Pier station, Nelson Street, in August 1960 on service No. 50, the destination showing "Market Place."

The protruding sign between 279 and the cyclist reads: "Booking office passengers and vehicles." There are also signs announcing a parcels office and the British Railways medical officer.

BELOW: Nowadays there are a host of different telephone and broadband providers but at the time of this picture, all public telephone services in Britain were provided by the Post Office - except, as one might expect, in Hull. This city had its own independent telephone network and still does. Consequently, this phone box on the Boulevard, where Corporation Transport AEC Regent No. 193 is calling with a Hull FC rugby special in August 1960, bears a white and blue colour scheme, not Post office red.

LEFT: Leyland TD7 Titan No. 203 being used by the City Engineer's department on Anlaby Road in September 1960. Classic cars form an incidental but important part of the street scenes and a Bond Minicar is prominent below right. Push-bikes and mopeds, as always, are also an integral part of the transport scene.

BELOW: AEC Regent No. 251 passes by the old Blundells warehouses on Spring Bank while approaching Ferensway with a No. 15 Bricknell Avenue service in August 1961. The top floor, a former paint works, was damaged by an accidental fire in 1940.

ABOVE: Daimler CVG6 No. 123, built in 1948, was with Newcastle Corporation until acquired by Hull along with nine others in 1961 to help replace the trolley buses. It is seen in King Edward Street in August 1962. These buses were all out of service by 1967.

BELOW: AEC Regent 111 No. 312 in Prospect Street with a No. 20 service in October 1964. In the distance is Blundell's Corner where Spring Bank goes to the left and Beverley Road to the right.

ABOVE: At Paragon before working service 98 to Hedon Road is AEC Regent 111 No. 107, one of a dozen 1949-built examples acquired from Leicester City Transport in 1966 and renumbered from 201-12 to 101-12. They were all withdrawn from service within three years.

BELOW: AEC Regent 111 No. 155 outside the Co-op in Prospect Street while on a 43B Preston Road service in May 1968. No. 155 was one of 36 1953/54 vintage vehicles with Park Royal bodywork acquired from Nottingham City Transport in 1967 and 1968. All were out of service by 1973. The building on the right ceased to be the Co-op but continued in traditional retail use by British Home Stores, although at the time of writing BHS - regarded like the Co-op as something of a national treasure - was in the process of being liquidated.

ABOVE: Leyland Panther No. 176 with Roe bodywork was one of five entering service in 1965. Here it is seen reversing with help from the police while preparing to pick up ferry passengers at Alexandra Dock West Jetty in 1971.

BELOW: This view of a very quiet Paragon Street in May 1937 shows East Yorkshire Leyland TD1 Titan No. 139 on a Withernsea service - to which it was dedicated judging by the legend on the side. No. 139 has an open staircase at the rear and notice the low, flat roof compared to the Corporation TD2 behind it. Posters on the right proclaim "the largest stock of musical instruments in the city" at the Paragon Music Stores.

ABOVE: Petrol driven EYMS Beverley Bar bus No. 275 in Paragon Square while setting out for Scarborough in May 1937. One can ponder at length about The Foot and Limb Centre above the chemist's on the left.

BELOW: Paragon Street in May 1937 with Leyland TD3 Titan No. 245 bound for Withernsea via Hedon aerodrome which from 1948 became a notable speedway racing venue. Built by Brush of Loughborough, 245 was too high for Beverley Bar and other low bridges which precluded it from going to York or Hornsea. The long-gone Yorkshire Herald claims to have all the scoops.

ABOVE: No. 245 again in Paragon Street in May 1937. Everyone looks very smartly dressed and the street is busy so it must be a Saturday afternoon - with wives in full control of their husbands. Above Suggs on the left a window proclaims The Humber Coal Co. Ltd., Coal Exporters, a symbol of the port's long lost past. Nowadays, with Britain's once massive coal industry virtually extinct despite plentiful reserves and ongoing demand, the coal is imported through Hull docks. Above the Corporation bus going away can be seen a sign proclaiming the offices of East Yorkshire Motor Services Ltd. Also visible in the scene is Meek's gent's hairdresser's - 8d for a cut - a funerary florists - "wreaths made to order" - the Kingston Tavern, and Henry Pickles newsagent. These 1930s street scenes give us a remarkable view of the old city centre before its destruction in world war two.

BELOW: EYMS No. 121 with a service to York via Beverley, Market Weighton and Pocklington at the top of Paragon Street in May 1937. No. 121 is a Leyland TS2 Tiger built in 1929 but rebuilt by Charles Roe in 1936. It had a single side-facing seat for the conductor at the back which the young author or his pals would try to grab, leaving the displeased conductor having to stand.

ABOVE: Never to be forgotten is the unusual roof profile of many of the double decker buses run by East Yorkshire and this June 1938 scene shows why. They were tailor-made to squeeze through the narrow medieval gate at Beverley and consequently were often referred as "Beverley Bar buses." Leyland No. 275 demonstrates just what a precise fit they were as it emerges from Beverley Bar with a Scarborough to Hull service. Nowadays buses follow a relief road and no longer pass through the bar.

BELOW: Leyland Titan No. 271 built in 1934 originally had a "Beverley Bar" roof until it caught fire in 1944, after which it was rebuilt by Willerbrook and given a flat roof. EYMS was short of low bridge buses at the time and so it was allocated to Elloughton where it was able to go under a low bridge carrying the Hull & Barnsley railway. Pictured in 1953 on the waste ground used as Paragon bus park, it was withdrawn three years later. The Corporation's tower vehicle can be seen in the left distance.

ABOVE: Paragon Square in the 1930s with East Yorkshire Leyland TD4 No. 301. The front destination blind shows it having arrived via Hesslewood, Boothferry Road and Barrow Lane.

BELOW: East Yorkshire No. 379 and driver wait at Paragon bus park to begin their run to Willerby Square via Derringham Bank and the golf course. No. 379 has a ribbed roof designed to reduce vibration but was the only one of the 1939-built GAT registered series not to be rebuilt with a new body. Behind it is No. 384, reg. GAT70, which was a rebuild.

ABOVE: As with Corporation Transport, East Yorkshire expanded by acquiring other operators and early 1950s AEC Regal No. 659 had been acquired along with Pocklington firm Everingham Bros. in 1953. Behind it is Beadle Leyland No. 562 in the primrose and mid blue livery which East Yorkshire applied to its coaches. No. 562 had been a double decker until rebuilt with an 8ft wide single decker body mounted on the original 7ft 6 in chassis. They are seen on 23rd May 1959 on the waste ground next to Paragon railway station that was used for bus parking and simply known as "The Waste."

BELOW: East Yorkshire also had Guy Arabs. No. 400, complete with Beverley Bar roof, is seen in Paragon Square at the corner of Carr Lane and Ferensway. Immediately above Reubens is Troxler and Stanley's restaurant window.

ABOVE: The primrose and mid-blue livery with chrome trims shows up well in this view of double deck coach No. 570 as it passes under the Hull & Barnsley Railway on Beverley Road in June 1956. The coaches were used on longer distance services. No. 570 was built by Leyland in 1952 with Roe bodywork. Because of its bright livery, it was often referred to as "The Yellow Peril." EYMS was still using a similar colour scheme on its coaches in 2016.

BELOW: Sister No. 573 passes through Beverley Bar on its way out of the town with a service from Hull to Leeds via Pocklington and York in August 1959.

ABOVE: 1950 Leylands 527 and flat roof 427 parked on The Waste in September 1957. No. 527 looks ready to go to Hornsea via Skirlaugh, Leven and Seaton, and 427 to South Cave via Boothferry Road. Between them is a West Yorkshire Road Car Co. single decker in red and cream livery which has arrived on a No. 46 service from Leeds via York, Pocklington and Beverley. This route was shared by the two operators at the time. Looming large is the north side of Paragon railway station which is now the bus station portion of Paragon Interchange.

BELOW: Beverley races have always brought many extra passengers for the buses. This amazing line-up of nine East Yorkshire double deckers waiting to leave Ferensway for the racecourse in July 1954 is headed by Leyland "Titan" No. 478.

ABOVE: 1957 AEC 30ft Regent No. 652 passes over Botanic Gardens level crossing while working a Cottingham via Willerby service in February 1958. Botanic Gardens signal box is on the right and the station on the left.

BELOW: 1944 Guy Arab No. 415 destined for Hessle Square passes sister No. 411 while turning off Anlaby Road into Midland Street in July 1958. On the left above No. 411 is another of those shops - selling, as the poster states: "Trusses, belts, all kinds of elastic hosiery, corsets, urinals, footwear to measure etc." Such shops would have been very necessary in the 1930s and 1950s given the hard, manual labour that was the norm in those days and the many war veterans with what are nowadays referred to as "life changing injuries." The bookie George Habbershaw had adverts on many buses. Ranged across behind the buses is the south side of Paragon railway station showing part of the original 1848 buildings, already in private use.

ABOVE: Guy Arab No. 406 crosses Drypool swing bridge in October 1958. The bridge was a cause of serious traffic congestion but was not rebuilt until 1959 when it was replaced with a Scherzer rolling lift bridge three times wider than that illustrated. The massive flour mills, built in 1952 to replace Joseph Rank's original 1875 mill which had been devastated in the blitz, were demolished in 2015/16.

BELOW: When the contest between road and rail at Hull's level crossings came to a head. East Yorkshire Leyland No. 475 attracts a crowd after colliding with the gates at Walton Street level crossing where the Bridlington line crosses Spring Bank West. The traffic lights which accompanied some of Hull's level crossings are at "stop." The conductor is trying to untangle the remains of the gate which has been broken in half, while 475 has a severely crumpled front mudguard.

ABOVE: New life for an old bus. Upon withdrawal from service, 1952-built AEC double decker reg. MKH 83 was cut down, converted to a recovery vehicle and re-registered as 270 AT, as seen outside Anlaby Road garage in 1972.

RIGHT: In the 1980s London Transport began selling off its iconic and long-serving AEC Routemaster buses, and between 1988 and 1993 several were acquired by East Yorkshire and placed on service 56. No. 809, built in 1963, is pictured in classic indigo and primrose livery at the Paragon bus park. *Stephen Chapman* Nos. 812, 816, 817 and 819 were subsequently converted to open top for the Scarborough seafront service. The last RM ran in regular service on Sunday 2nd September 2001 but No. 812 is retained as part of the EYMS heritage fleet.

ABOVE: On Saturday 3rd August 1991 the doors of East Yorkshire's main garage in Anlaby Road were opened to reveal three classics that were part of the company's heritage fleet. On the left is AEC "Beverley Bar Bus" No. 644 and on the right, AEC Regent No. T1, used for driver training, both restored to the classic EYMS livery which had been out of general use since the 1970s. In the centre is Leyland PD3 No. 602 converted to open top for the Scarborough sea front service. The EYMS fleet had undergone renumbering since the earlier pages in this book. *Stephen Chapman*

LEFT: In the 1980s the Bristol VRTs became a standard EYMS double decker. No. 519, prepared for a run to Hornsea, is seen on the Paragon bus park in the 1990s. With the National Bus Company abolished, the old livery makes a comeback.
Stephen Chapman

ABOVE: A reminder that Hull, like every city, is constantly changing. This August 1998 view of an East Yorkshire Bristol VRT turning into Carlton Street and making for Paragon bus station, has changed dramatically since then. Paragon House on the left, the railway office block which replaced Paragon railway station's large Edwardian portico frontage in 1962, has since been demolished, while the cinema building opposite, has been replaced by a large new shopping centre along with the large, dark and unwelcoming shed that was Paragon bus station. A new bus interchange has been incorporated into the railway station's redundant north side. The last of the VRTs was withdrawn in 2004. In 2016 much of the EYMS fleet comprises Volvo vehicles along with such other makes as Alexander Dennis and M.A.N. *Stephen Chapman*

RIGHT: Among all the city centre delivery vehicles milling about were the Hull Brewery Company's drays delivering essential supplies to the city's pubs. Its horse-drawn drays were a familiar and much-loved sight up to the 1970s, which is when this one is seen during a routine delivery with drayman and magnificent shire "Prince."
Robert Anderson

LEFT: Where it all began. Before the days of trams and motor buses, bus services were provided by horse-drawn omnibuses like this one found in a farmyard in Aldbrough in 1957. It had been used on a service into Hull until 1922 when it was known as "Mr. Collinson's Tankabus."

BELOW: How the docks have changed - not just in Hull but everywhere. This view taken from the public footpath that went along the roofs of warehouses, shows a congested and cluttered scene at the Riverside Quay on Wednesday 14th June 1961. Before the era of containers and bulk loads, what in those days were heavy lorries, tow tractors, even cars mingle with all kinds of loose cargoes - mostly exports - laid out on the dockside and requiring a great deal of manual handling. The railway vans being loaded are for the 5.50pm Mondays Only bacon train to Manchester Oldham Road. On the right is Albert Dock. Towards the bottom right of the picture a tow tractor is trying to thread its way through the jam.
Peter Rose

ON THE RAILS. *Until the 1960s, Hull's railways consisted of two distinct systems, those lines that had belonged to the North Eastern Railway, and those which had originated with the Hull & Barnsley Railway. Together they formed an extensive and complex network that reached all across the city. It included inner and outer suburban passenger stations, 20 goods and coal depots, nine railway-served docks, over 40 private sidings, three major locomotive depots, a locomotive works and, in the west, vast freight marshalling yards.*

The first railway reached Hull in 1840 when a through route from Leeds was established by opening of the Hull & Selby Railway which followed the north bank of the estuary and terminated alongside Kingston Street, just short of Humber Dock. The Hull & Selby was then leased to the York & North Midland Railway while a branch from Dairycoates to Cottingham and Bridlington was added in 1846, extending to Seamer and thus forming a through route to Scarborough in 1847. A year later the Kingston Street terminus was replaced by Paragon station along with new lines off the Bridlington branch at Hessle Road and Cottingham South. The adjoining Royal Station Hotel opened for business in 1851. In the early 1900s Paragon station was massively extended with the magnificent arched trainshed roof we see today.

In 1850 the Hull Dock Company completed Victoria Dock, east of the city, to accommodate larger vessels than was possible at the existing town docks, and so the Y&NMR followed suit with a branch to the new dock completed in 1853 from the Hessle Road-Paragon line at Anlaby Road. The dock branch required six level crossings over city streets, a swing bridge over the river Hull, and another swing bridge within the dock area itself - plus a flat crossing over the Paragon-Cottingham line. In years to come, the amount of time the level crossing gates were closed due to the sheer volume of rail traffic would be a source of delay and irritation to all road users. And they were not the only level crossings to bedevil Hull - it once had to 22 of them.

In 1854 the Y&NMR became part of the newly formed North Eastern Railway. Railways that were initially owned by independent locally-promoted concerns were opened from the Victoria Dock branch to Withernsea and Hornsea in 1854 and 1864 respectively, the former using a station at Victoria Dock for the first ten years. In 1865 the NER completed its

So far as many visitors to Hull were concerned, Paragon station was all of its railway and they might only have fleeting glimpses of the lines that spread across the city to reach the docks like the roots of a tree searching for water. This amazing scene in the late 1940s shows almost the full extent of the station with carriage sidings on the left and, beyond them through the smog, Paragon bus station. Class D20 4-4-0 No. 62348 is leaving with a service to Selby as K3 2-6-0 No. 61935 blows off surplus steam while awaiting departure with an express. Various tank engines can be seen on pilot duty in the background. The view is from Park Street bridge which, when built in 1871, was the first in the city to replace a level crossing. *Tom Greaves*

line through the Wolds from Beverley to Market Weighton, opening up the direct route to York.

The NER and the Hull Dock Co. had a complete monopoly of all traffic through the port which local businesses found to be against their interests. Backed by the Corporation they decided to introduce competition by building their own dock and railway. This they called The Hull, Barnsley & West Riding Junction Railway and Dock Co., later shortened to the Hull & Barnsley Railway. After a protracted and costly construction, the new Alexandra Dock and main line through the Wolds to the West Riding had been completed by 1885. The H&B line encircled the northern suburbs of Hull on embankments, crossing the streets by means of bridges. The company sited its main workshops and locomotive depot at Springhead and built a branch down to a goods station at Neptune Street, by the riverside docks, west of the city. The H&B only managed to reach the outskirts of Barnsley but at Cudworth it had a junction with the Midland Railway's main line from Carlisle to London. It's promoters had, however, achieved their aim of gaining direct access to the Yorkshire Coalfield and carrying coal to Alexandra Dock for shipping was its main business - along with timber pit props in the returning wagons - until closure as a through route came in 1958. The H&B also carried passengers and had a station in Cannon Street, at the end of a branch off the main line. In the early 20th century the H&B's passenger service included Hull-Sheffield expresses for which five truly elegant 4-4-0 engines were built.

In the early 1900s, Hull found itself on the front line of a European migrant crisis and an operation that would be a lesson to Europe in the 2015/16 crisis went into action. Some 75,000 refugees, mainly jews fleeing persecution in eastern Europe, and most heading for America, arrived at Hull by the shipload. Special trains to Liverpool for trans-Atlantic sailings were organised by various railway companies over every conceivable route. Facilities that dealt with the migrants included an H&B station at Alexandra Dock Landing Stage, an NER station at the Riverside Quay, and a building by Paragon station where they were processed, fed and medically checked before continuing to Liverpool. The building and an excursion platform that was utilized survive to this day.

Despite bitter rivalry between them, the NER and H&B actually joined forces to build a new jointly-owned deep water dock at the eastern extremity near Marfleet. King George Dock was opened in 1914 along with an oil import jetty at Saltend and a connecting joint line from both the H&B and NER lines. Today it is Hull's principal dock.

After the 1923 Grouping of the country's many railway companies into the Big Four, all of Hull's railways came under the London & North Eastern Railway. They were then nationalised in 1948 to form British Railways. The LNER wasted no time in trying to combine the two systems. It opened a new curve off the H&B line at Spring Bank North down to the Bridlington line at Walton Street in 1924, enabling H&B passenger trains to use Paragon station, Cannon Street being relegated to a goods depot. But ambitious plans to eliminate the Victoria Dock line and its level crossings did not materialise and nothing changed until 1968, after withdrawal of the Hornsea and Withernsea passenger services, the line closing when new connections allowed all docks traffic to use the H&B route.

Hull's railways underwent many changes over the years - first expansion and then, from the 1950s, rapid decline to the point where in 2016 the extent of railway in the city is virtually back to what it was in 1848 with only the Selby and Scarborough lines remaining open, plus the H&B line from King George Dock to Hessle Road, where it was joined to the NER line in 1962.

The Hull & Barnsley Railway built its line to Alexandra Dock on a high level, avoiding the need for level crossings which handicapped the North Eastern's Victoria Dock line. This view on 15th July 1959 shows a J39 0-6-0 heading petrol tanks from Saltend along the H&B in east Hull, having just passed Burleigh Street signal box and goods yard. The Hornsea branch passes underneath on the left.

ABOVE: Hull's premier train was its Pullman to London King's Cross which ran as through coaches attached at Doncaster to the Harrogate-King's Cross Yorkshire Pullman. Here, class V3 2-6-2 tank No. 67640 awaits departure with the Hull portion which it will work as far as Doncaster. In 1967 the Pullman started running as full length separate train called The Hull Pullman, until superseded in May 1978 by The Hull Executive, an ordinary InterCity train with Pullman-style service in first class.

BELOW: The prolific D49 "Shire" and "Hunt" class 4-4-0s designed by Sir Nigel Gresley were a class of locomotive very familiar to the Hull area before diesels took their place, being used on both express and local passenger services. No. 62727 *The Quorn* heads the 8.45am to King's Cross past Hessle Road and underneath the Hull & Barnsley line from Neptune Street to Springhead on 2nd October 1959. The D49 will doubtless hand over to a Pacific at Doncaster. Behind the bridge are Hessle Road signal box, level crossing and footbridge. The D49s were allocated almost exclusively to Yorkshire and Scotland. In summer 1960 the already redundant Yorkshire-based survivors were brought out of storage at Springhead engine shed to help with heavy summer traffic, after which they were all withdrawn for scrap. One Scottish engine, No. 62712 *Morayshire,* has been preserved.

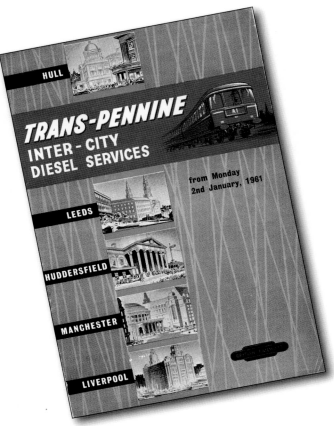

Since the start of the 20th century trans-Pennine trains had linked Hull and Liverpool. In January 1961 specially-designed "Trans-Pennine" inter-city diesel multiple units built at Swindon and equipped with high-powered Rolls Royce engines replaced steam. They featured high-backed armchair seats and curtains in second class, open plan and compartment coaches, and a buffet car with a griddle serving hot food including the "Angus", a burger made from finest Aberdeen Angus beef. They also carried roof boards proclaiming "Trans-Pennine" and "Liverpool-Hull." After a short initial spell based at Leeds, they were all allocated to Botanic Gardens depot.

The new service comprised five Hull-Liverpool trains each way per day while overall journey times were cut by an average of 45 minutes. In the leaflet opposite, BR described the Trans-Pennines as a "giant's stride forwards."

In May 1979 British Rail axed the Hull-Liverpool service and the Trans-Pennines, minus buffet cars, were relegated to Hull-Leeds and relatively slow Hull-Sheffield-Manchester runs for what remained of their days. In time the service returned and forms today's Hull-Manchester Trans-Pennine Express formed of German-built 3-car trains running every hour.

On Sunday 23rd March 1980 and nearing the end of its days, a Trans-Pennine leaves Paragon with the 17.00 to Manchester Piccadilly via Sheffield. The canopies on the right form part of the original 1848 station while the big trainshed, evidently in need of some repair at this time, was completed in 1904. *Stephen Chapman*

ABOVE: Just as today, expresses to London and Manchester shared the route out of Hull with stopping trains to Selby and Doncaster. This somewhat paradoxical 1958 view shows the 2.50pm Leeds stopping service being headed past St. George's Road crossing, between Anlaby Road and Hessle Road, by an engine more likely to be used on an express. It is A3 Pacific No. 60086 *Gainsborough*.

BELOW: More usual motive power for Hull local services in the days of steam. On 29th July 1951, A6 4-6-2 tank No. 69791 waits at Paragon station with a train to Hornsea or Withernsea. These engines were rebuilt by the NER from 4-6-0 tanks originally intended for the Scarborough-Whitby line and nicknamed "Whitby Willies."

ABOVE: The former North Eastern class R 4-4-0s, classed D20 by the LNER and BR, were staple power for local and even some express services until the second half of the 1950s, most working to Hull from other depots. This view, captured shortly after nationalisation in 1948, shows Selby-based E2386 at Paragon station. The E prefix was applied to the LNER number until BR's own numbering system with a 6 prefix for ex-LNER engines was finalised. *Tom Greaves*

BELOW: From the late 1950s the most common form of power for those passenger trains that were still steam were undoubtably the B1 4-6-0s. Here in February 1966, No. 61406, based across the water at Immingham, prepares to work the 08.52 to Doncaster, one of the last steam passenger trains from Hull. *Peter Rose*

ABOVE: The direct line to York via Market Weighton carried a mixture of local and express passenger services and goods traffic until its closure in November 1965. In later years it was largely diesel-operated but until 1964 it was the stamping ground of the last B16 4-6-0s, a type which originated on the NER in 1909. No. 61444, rebuilt as class B16/3 in the 1940s, leaves Paragon with the mid-day parcels train to York on 24th April 1959. This train was the return working of the 8.14am stopping passenger from York.

BELOW: But for a local service as far as South Howden which lasted until 1955, the Hull & Barnsley passenger service was withdrawn in 1932. The H&B's attractive 4-4-0 express engines - classed by the LNER as D24 - had already been re-assigned to other local passenger services and transferred from Springhead to Botanic Gardens shed in 1924. No. 2426 is seen at Paragon station with just such a local service on Saturday 4th November 1933, the final month of its life.

ABOVE: Class A6 4-6-2T No. 69796 with a local service at Paragon in 1948. When withdrawn in March 1953 it was the last survivor of a class once so familiar on Hornsea and Withernsea services. *Tom Greaves*

BELOW: It goes without saying that fish from Hull was once a major source of rail traffic with block trains running from the fish docks west of the city to London and across the country. Fish was also taken by rail from the docks to Paragon station for forwarding by passenger and parcels train and road delivery. Here, J94 class 0-6-0 saddle tank No. 68011, a wartime Austerity design built for the Ministry of Supply in large numbers by various manufacturers, is at the original 1848 portion of Paragon station on 11th November 1958. It has just brought trip working No. 133 conveying fish vans for attachment to the 1.20pm Scarborough train.

ABOVE: Local passenger services were also powered by G5 0-4-4 tanks prior to replacement by diesel units in the second half of the 1950s but here, one day in 1958, No. 67263 has been assigned to station pilot duty.

My earliest encounter with railways came in Willerby during the war. For a time we lived with my grandparents. My grandad had been a builder and he had a big double decker building at the back of the house - it's still there actually. There were steps up the outside to a little landing and the joiners' shop. I used to stand on the landing and watch the trains go by as we were right alongside Willerby station. In the lower part of the building were stables which extended right underneath the railway embankment, and during air raids we'd go right to the back of the stables and under the straw. We could hear the horses chuntering and panting two or three stalls down and we felt safe there.

In 1947 I got a scholarship to Hymers College and had to go for an exam to see if I was good enough. As we got off the bus at the adjacent Botanic Gardens level crossing I saw an old Great Northern Railway 4-4-0, a D2 - No. 2193 I think, coming over the crossing with a train from Withernsea. Botanic Gardens engine shed was in view of Hymers and just at the time I started there an engine was delivered new to Botanic. It was B1 4-6-0 No. 61306 and so I always had a particular affection for this engine. It was among the last steam locos to work in Hull and has thankfully been preserved.

In summer 1953 the engine shed at Mexborough, between Doncaster and Sheffield, acquired a couple of "Large Director" 4-4-0s, Nos. 62666 Zeebrugge and 62667 Somme. As a result they came to Hull and worked out on the 4.13pm to Liverpool Central so I'd leave school at 4 o'clock and run like blazes down Derringham Street until I reached Argyle Street bridge, just in time to see one coming out of Paragon.

Sometimes my mother and I would go into town on the bus and go for a walk to Victoria Pier to see the ferries. As we came to Monument Bridge, the old entrance to Queen's Dock, and over to Whitefriargate, we had Prince's dock on the right where a firm, C. D. Holmes I think it was, used to fit out trawlers with engines, so we'd usually see a couple of trawlers there. There was also Stevens' little ice cream cart and just beyond that the start of Prince's Dock siding where there were nearly always a couple of railway goods vans appearing to stand in the road. This was the first time I had ever come so close to anything to do with railways. Before that I always saw them from a distance or while on a platform. But on Prince's Dock side you were looking up at these things and they were enormous. No locomotives were allowed down there because the only rail access was via the little bridge over the lock gates at the entrance to Humber Dock, and it was too weak to take locomotives. Instead they used a "tow motor" - a tractor adapted for pushing railway wagons. There were single storey wooden warehouses along there and once when there was a gas leak, some fool dropped a cigarette. The whole lot went up, wagons and all. It was a hell of a blaze. At the far side of Humber Dock was another warehouse and I remember seeing that going up in flames. When we got back later they'd put the fire out and all that was left was a door and on the door it said in large letters: "In case of fire ring 33303." I thought that was brilliant.

Then I started going to Paragon spotting at weekends. Once in 1950, a Scarborough train was coming in pulled by a most strange looking engine. In fact it was class A5 4-6-2 tank No. 69839 running bunker first - a type we didn't have

51

in Hull at the time. I think it must have worked from Middlesbrough to Scarborough, and Scarborough were short of power so they grabbed it and sent it to Hull. On another occasion I saw "Shire" 4-4-0 Banffshire come in and thought "What the hell's that doing here?" I went back to school and said "I've just seen Banffshire and everyone said "You liar." It was a Scottish engine but "Hunt" class No. 2743 The Cleveland had been swapped for it.

When I got loose on my own I started going over the Humber Dock lock gates, beyond which was a street that went to a place called "T" Bridge, over the end of the little freight yard at Railway Dock. Then, when I was 15 I went to the dock offices at the top of Queen's Gardens and got a permit to go on all the docks - by signing my life away over a sixpenny stamp. The world was then my oyster. I'd walk along Prince's Dock, Humber Dock, over the lock gates and through the main gate into Albert Dock where I would start photographing. The police never bothered me because I

Manor House was the end of the running line from Dairycoates West to the various riverside docks and goods depots, and close to the old Hull & Selby Railway terminus. J77 No. 68413 waits next to the signal box while on No. 7 pilot duty in August 1953. The shunting engines used as pilots would be on site for a week at a time, only returning to the engine shed at weekends, so the crew needed to get home from wherever the engine was, hence the driver's bike tied to the handrail.

Beyond here sidings went into Hull Central and Railway Street goods yards, and also by lifting bridge over the entrance to Humber Dock, along Humber Dock and Prince's Dock streets - a section where locomotives did not venture - shunting being carried out by horses or tractors - and at one time across Alfred Gelder Street to Queens Dock, terminating just short of High Street.

had a permit. Shortly after the lock gates, on the left, was a Great Central Railway trespass warning notice which I thought rather odd in Hull. Behind the wall was what we called the "old wharf" which was the goods equivalent of Corporation Pier, served by lighters from new Holland and originally belonging to the GC. I was also at the point to which locomotives were allowed to work. I'd walk from there to William Wright Dock and eventually to the fish dock which was a marvellous place. There were so many trawlers that you could just about walk across the dock over their decks. At the top end of the fish dock extension was a slipway where they'd draw trawlers up for repairs.

In those days, 1952/53, so much was going on, especially with all the railway that was there and there were all sorts of engines, such as J71 and J77 tanks on pilots, N8s and N10s knocking about shunting, and freights coming in.

The eastern docks were equally interesting. You'd set off to walk down Alfred Gelder Street and that led to Drypool Bridge. Over that you'd turn right and continue to Citadel Street, by the end of which you were coming across timber bogies in the middle of the road because there were rails everywhere. It was a haunt of Sentinel steam locos and I would get footplate trips on them. One day, we were pushing a load of "No go greens" - old 10-ton common user wagons that they used to say "not to leave the dock." They'd load them with timber and push them around the place. We were pushing this load and I was hanging out of the cab watching it go round the corner when suddenly the wagons started tipping over, buffer-locked, and I thought "my God, this lot's coming over and if it comes over I'm

going to go with it." I said to the driver
"Whoa! We've got a buffer-lock on."

"Oh damn," he said and put the anchors on, just reversed the Sentinel and released the jammed buffers.

From there you could go through to Alexandra Dock where there were engine sidings where all these locos would stand at weekends. There were J77s and an N13 for a while, No. 69111 acting as the Saltend pilot which was heavy work.

When I finished school I went to Dairycoates engine shed as a fitter's apprentice which was a disaster because I've never been any good at anything mechanical. I recall going there one day and the foreman saying: "You're going with so and so to work on such and such and loco and the donkey pump's packed up." The donkey pump? I went outside and there, in green was No. 61611 Rainham Hall. Anyway, we dealt with the donkey pump with the usual "Derby screwdriver" - in other words we belted it with a 7lb mallet and it started working again.

We all had a great system going there. We got what were called "X repairs" - a card we were given showing all the repairs to be done on a loco. Only we'd skive off to the canteen at 3 o'clock, drink tea and eat toast so the job didn't get done by 4.15 when we were supposed to knock off. The foreman had to say: "We'll have to do half a shift to finish the job because we want the engine in steam tonight." So then we'd go back and finish the job in half an hour and get paid up to 8 o'clock. A great fiddle.

"We'd have the Sentinels to repair. When you'd done the work you had to light it up. Now a Sentinel took only about an hour and three quarters to come to the boil because it was only a small boiler. We'd light the fire at 11am so it came to the boil about half past twelve. Dinner hour was 12 - 1pm and if you were looking after a Sentinel you had to stay with the job to make sure the water didn't run dry or anything, so we used to claim for the lunch hour and get paid and hour and a quarter pay on tops. I actually couldn't get extra pay so I was allowed to leave early. Dairycoates was a cold place to work. You'd freeze solid trying to replace the chains on a Sentinel on a winter's day. Changing a bike chain is bad enough in the freezing cold but imagine doing that six times over - with grease.

I went to Springhead for a couple of months. I was on diesel shunters and remember driving one on the shed. It went round the corner and "bang," I'd hit another shunter. The foreman came rushing out "What the *!#! hell's going on here!" I was never allowed to drive again.

The author was one of an enthusiast team who spent the whole of Christmas 1963 camped at the former H&B Sculcoates goods yard where Messrs. Albert Draper were about to start cutting up withdrawn BR steam locomotives. Among the ill-fated was B16 4-6-0 No. 61420 and their aim was to polish it up in order that it could face the cutter's torch with dignity. Pictured on 12th January 1964, 61420 was the first BR steam locomotive cut up by Drapers and up to 1969 no less than 732 locomotives met their ultimate fate at this and their later site in Neptune Street goods yard.

On Hull's suburban network.

LEFT: In the early days of British Railways, a class B stopping train to Hornsea or Withernsea approaches Botanic Gardens station under the charge of J39 0-6-0 No. 64939. A goods train bound for the docks waits its turn on the line from Anlaby Road. *Tom Greaves*

BELOW: Various types of tank and small tender engines were deployed on local passenger services around Hull in the post-war years. Nearly new class L1 2-6-4T No. 67766, a class introduced in 1945, waits at Stepney station, Beverley Road, with a 1950s service to Hornsea or Withernsea.

RIGHT: Wilmington was the junction where the Hornsea branch parted company from the line to Withernsea and the docks. A Cravens-built diesel multiple unit calls at Wilmington station which had been relocated in 1912 and built on a raised level, hence the timber construction.

These diesel units based at Botanic Gardens were commonplace on Hull services until the early 1980s. They were notorious for the way interior fittings constantly rattled.

BELOW: On what might be termed Hull's outer suburban. In August 1962 the 5.16pm express from York pulls into Cottingham station hauled by B1 4-6-0 No. 61084. Cottingham remains open for business in 2016 but alas without the York trains.

ABOVE: An A6 4-6-2T hauls a Withernsea or Hornsea express composed of venerable coaches through the eastern outskirts of Hull in the late 1940s. The engine is yet to receive its BR front number plate while the number painted on its buffer beam is totally obscured by grime. *Tom Greaves*

BELOW: A 1951 summer holiday bike ride has been brought to a halt by Botanic Gardens level crossing while A6 No. 69796 calls at the station with a service from Hornsea or Withernsea. Will the cyclists be calling at Duggleby's Cycles when they finally get on the move? A poster left of the wicket gate on the left advertises a special excursion fare to see Hull City play at Sheffield United on 25th August, which the Tigers lost 4-1.

ABOVE: Another outer suburban station still open for business today is Hessle, on the line to Selby and Doncaster, although it looks very different as the slow lines have been removed and the platforms extended out to the two remaining fast lines. On Wednesday 14th March 1962, K3 2-6-0 No. 61899 storms through at the head of the mid-day express to King's Cross. No. 61899 was the last K3 to receive an overhaul. These engines were an integral part of the Hull railway scene on both goods and passenger trains until mass withdrawal in winter 1962/63.

BELOW: Engines originating with railway companies alien to Hull were frequent visitors. From the territory of the former London Midland & Scottish Railway, 4F 0-6-0 No. 44274 of Royston shed near Barnsley, heads a train of empty hopper wagons westbound through Hessle in May 1957. Given the likely destination of this train one might have expected it to be running via the Hull & Barnsley line.

ABOVE: Memorable among Hull's outer suburban services were the trains which ran each day to and from Brough for workers at Blackburn's aircraft factory. This daily spectacular at Brough with two trains departing simultaneously, both of them the 5.15pm to Hull, was captured on Thursday 22nd August 1963. The train on the left hauled by V3 2-6-2T No. 67638 is a fast train and that on the right headed by V3 No. 67684 is the slow train. *Peter Rose*

BELOW: Into the outer suburbs on the Withernsea branch. B1 4-6-0 No. 61002 *Impala* leads the Hedon pick-up goods back towards Hull from the closed Marfleet station on Friday 18th March 1966. The overbridge being crossed by a Corporation double decker on Marfleet Lane replaced a level crossing in the 1930s. *Rev. David Benson*

Not to be overlooked are those suburban stations on the Hull & Barnsley Railway.

RIGHT: The first station after leaving Cannon Street was Beverley Road, the busiest station on the H&B. This street-side view on 27th August 1983, shortly before demolition, shows the substantial station building with the railway embankment behind, the platforms having been at first floor level. Beverley Road closed completely and Cannon Street to passengers in 1924 when H&B passenger trains were rerouted to Paragon.

BELOW: The next station, out in the suburbs(after the small timber halt at Springhead) was Willerby & Kirkella which closed to passengers in 1955 when the Hull-South Howden service was axed and the H&B became freight only.

This 1951 view shows ex-Great Northern Railway C12 4-4-2T No. 67397 arriving with what is thought to be the 11.45am Saturdays Only Hull to South Howden. *P. N. Williams*

Given its position at the end of a main line from the West Riding and at a point where lines radiated to the Yorkshire coast, it should come as no surprise that Hull, far from being the end of the line, was something of a hub for excursion trains bound for the various seaside resorts and especially Butlin's holiday camp at Filey which had its own station.

ABOVE: Summer excursions for Bridlington, Filey Holiday Camp and Scarborough could avoid a reversal in Hull by taking the original Hull & Selby line from Hessle Road to Cottingham South, otherwise known as the Newington Branch or the "Straight Line." This view shows BR Standard class 3 2-6-0 No. 77012 on that line while passing Waterworks level crossing with an inspection saloon. This engine survived in use at York until June 1967 as a regular for saloon duties.

BELOW: B1 4-6-0 No. 61111 has just passed Hessle with a summer Sunday excursion from the Sheffield area to Bridlington on 12th July 1959.

ABOVE: A 1950s excursion from Scarborough approaches Paragon station headed by D49 "Shire" class 4-4-0 No. 62701 *Derbyshire*. *Tom Greaves*

BELOW: The day *Flying Scotsman* came to Hull. On Saturday 6th April 1968 it passes round the so-called Cricket Ground Curve with an excursion from Birmingham. When this curve, from Anlaby Road Junction to West Parade Junction, was installed in 1965, it enabled closure of the original Hull & Selby line between Hessle Road and Cottingham South, eliminating three level crossings in the process, as well as providing an alternative route to the Selby-Driffield line which had closed in June 1965. Today the Cricket Ground Curve epithet is no longer relevant as the cricket ground on the right has been superseded by the KC Stadium. *Rev. David Benson*

ABOVE: No. 61452, one of the original NER class S3 4-6-0s(classed B16/1 by the LNER and BR,) crosses the Beverley line on 12th July 1959 as it heads along the Victoria Dock branch at Victoria Crossing with a special taking soldiers from Penistone to a training camp near Hornsea Bridge. The author climbed a signal post for this shot and with the train being late, was up there for 30 minutes - without being challenged.

BELOW: The very occasional railway enthusiasts' special would be allowed to provide its complement of "gricers" with the rare treat of a ride over Hull's various freight only dock lines, and still does. This Railway Correspondence & Travel Society diesel railtour is at Alexandra Dock on 10th October 1964. Alexandra Dock signal box, pictured here, was the biggest on the H&B but closed in 1974. The whole railway, by then hardly used, was removed when the dock closed in 1983 and was not reinstated when the dock reopened.
D. P. Leckonby

Paragon station and its passenger trains may have been the public face of Hull's railways but there was so much more that went unseen, at least by the casual visitor if not by residents and workers. That was, of course, the mindboggling amount of goods traffic that passed through marshalling yards in west Hull on its way to and from the docks, goods stations and various industrial concerns. Every conceivable commodity was carried by train until the 1960s whereas in 2016 goods traffic is limited to steel, scrap metal and imported coal and biomass through the docks, and stone to a terminal at Dairycoates. Practically all else goes by road.

ABOVE: The freight side had its premier expresses, one qualifying for a name. That was 6.50pm "Humber-Clyde" fully braked express from Hull to Glasgow. It is seen setting off from Outward Yard on 13th May 1964 under the charge of York-based double-chimneyed V2 2-6-2 No. 60963. Just as often used on express passenger trains, these engines were designed by Sir Nigel Gresley for express goods trains such as this and were known as the "Green Arrows" after class pioneer *Green Arrow* which was named after the LNER's Green Arrow express goods service. None were based in Hull and one was worked from York each day specially for this train. *Peter Rose*

BELOW: Next in the express goods pecking order perhaps, was the 7.35pm to Washwood Heath, Birmingham, seen leaving the Outward Yard behind B1 4-6-0 No. 61176 on the same evening as above. Overseeing the departure is inspector Jack Wilby who served with the army on the railways of Iran and Italy during the second world war. The 350hp diesel shunter on the right is No. 19 pilot in the fish sidings. Its name leaving no doubt, the Outward Yard was where outgoing trains leaving Hull were marshalled together. *Peter Rose*

ABOVE: Just to show that anything could happen in Hull. Another notable freight was the 7.30am to Stockton, seen here on 1st June 1960 in a scene that is wholly incongruous. What amounts to a train of empty coal wagons storms through Hessle on the fast line hauled by a locomotive as high status as high status can be. Streamlined A4 Pacific No. 60019 *Bittern* would normally be hauling high speed expresses on the East Coast main line and these illustrious engines were rarely seen in Hull, but it should not be overlooked that they were also designed to haul freight.

BELOW: High ranking among the freight trains coming out of Hull were, of course, the fish trains. This one, again passing through Hessle, on 14th June 1959 is being hauled by K3 2-6-0 No. 61813. In their heyday up to eight fish trains a day ran from Hull to all parts of the country - and then there were individual vans attached to other passenger and parcels trains. In steam days Hessle station was a popular location for photographers and spotters.

ABOVE: In BR days the B16 4-6-0s of all versions were generally shared out between York and Leeds Neville Hill depots with a solitary example at Scarborough and a handful of migrants to foreign territory at Mirfield in the West Riding. In December 1962, however, some were transferred from York to Hull Dairycoates to become the last members of this fine and historic class in service until withdrawn in 1964. Here in 1963, B16/2 No. 61463, rebuilt in the 1930s to Sir Nigel Gresley's design, blasts through Hessle on the Up Slow line with empty coal wagons for the West Riding. At one time millions of tons of coal were exported through Hull each year but, ironically, power station coal and new fuel biomass are now imported, and so it is loaded trains that pass westbound through Hessle.

BELOW: The docks, depots and private sidings were connected to the main yards by a network of humble but vital trip workings, each one identified by a number displayed on a tablet carried by the engine, while the many pilots that did the shunting at the various locations were similarly numbered. The following pictures illustrate some of these trip workings and pilots in numerical order. Here, with the "Billingsgate" fish markets of St. Andrew's Dock on the right, BR Standard class 3 2-6-0 No. 77002 works trip No. J03 of loaded fish vans from the dock exchange sidings to the Outward Yard on Monday 22nd July 1963. *Peter Rose*

ABOVE: BR class 3 2-6-0 No. 77002 heads trip J04, consisting of empty coal wagons, westbound along the former Hull & Barnsley line at Spring Bank North on Tuesday 16th April 1963. The signal protects the junction with the line down to Walton Street. *Peter Rose*

LEFT: A pair of Paxman diesels cross the Wilmington swing bridge carrying the Victoria Dock branch over the River Hull with a trip from Hessle quarry on Thursday 20th July 1967. This double track bridge replaced the original narrow version with interlaced tracks in 1906. The fully restored and working bridge survives today and carries a public footpath.
Rev. David Benson

Built at Swindon from 1964, the Paxman locomotives were meant for use on trip and branch line goods trains on the Western Region of BR. But by the time they were delivered much of their intended work had gone and they were redundant almost from the start. They were sent to Hull to replace the area's last steam engines on the trip workings but while they achieved that aim, they were not a success. They had to be used in pairs to provide enough brake power and because they were not equipped for multiple working each one required a crew which was expensive. They ended up being sold, primarily to the coal and steel industries where they managed at last to find a useful role.

RIGHT: Trip J07's itinerary included two daily sorties up what remained of the Hull & Barnsley line to Little Weighton, and it is seen on that line alongside a North Eastern Railway slotted post signal while shunting the returning last revenue-earning train at Willerby & Kirkella on Friday 3rd July 1964.

The engine is B1 4-6-0 No. 61306 which on Saturday 27th November 1965 was given another last train to haul. That was to York over the direct route via Market Weighton, the 7.30pm from Paragon. No. 61306 ended its BR service in the West Riding, and when withdrawn in September 1967 was preserved and given the name *Mayflower* which had previously been carried by Lincolnshire-based sister 61379. *Peter Rose*

BELOW: Working Trip J07 on Friday 4th June 1965, WD 2-8-0 No. 90044 heads along the Bridlington line towards Walton Street while conveying ferry vans with exports from the Ideal factory in the right background. Thanks to the newly installed Cricket Ground Curve the train has a direct route to the marshalling yards. *Peter Rose*

ABOVE: On Saturday 11th July 1964 WD 2-8-0 No. 90450 stands alongside St. Andrews Dock West signal box while on Trip J08 duty. Behind it, fellow WD No. 90711 waits to take up the 6.45pm Saturdays Only to Laisterdyke, Bradford. *Peter Rose*

BELOW: B1 No. 61306 has charge this time of J13 duty and is seen in the exchange sidings between the NER and H&B systems at Albert Dock on Friday 24th July 1964 while running round its train before taking it to the Outward Yard. No. 61012 *Puku* in the background has arrived in order to undergo a similar manoeuvre. The new curve laid from the H&B to Hessle Road in 1962 eliminated much of the need for trains to reverse here but some still had to run round in order to reach the Outward Yard. The sidings on the extreme right rejoiced in the rather odd name of "New Found Out Sidings." *Peter Rose*
In the early years of the H&B such was the antipathy between it and the NER that this spot was more like a sensitive international frontier with rarely opened padlocked gates separating the two.

ABOVE: With dockyard cranes ranged across the skyline, WD 2-8-0 No. 90378 working Trip J14 pulls away from Alexandra Dock, over Hedon Road and on to the H&B high level line with tanks from the BP complex at Saltend. *Rev. David Benson*

BELOW: Trip J16 behind WD 2-8-0 No. 90272 also has tanks from Saltend as it passes King George Dock Junction on Wednesday 1st March 1967. *Rev. David Benson*

ABOVE: On the high lines at King George Dock Junction, WD 2-8-0 No. 90352 works J19 trip bringing empty mineral wagons from the coal shipping berths towards Alexandra Dock and the H&B line on Saturday 21st January 1967. J19 also went to the cement works at Melton. *Rev. David Benson*

BELOW: The policeman on point duty is momentarily distracted by the progress of K3 2-6-0 No. 61857 as it passes over Botanic Gardens level crossing on 8th August 1962 with J19 duty. The engine has a former Great Northern Railway tender.

ABOVE: Ivatt 2-6-2T No. 41262 passes Dairycoates East on Tuesday 28th May 1963 while on Trip J22, leaving St. Andrew's Dock at 11am for Paragon station with fish for passenger train-rated transit. This whole area of extensive sidings all the way to Manor House has been swallowed up by the Clive Sullivan Way trunk road and new development. St. Andrews fish dock has been allowed to silt up and return to nature. Shipping still uses Albert Dock and William Wright Dock, but all that remains of the railway are disused rails embedded in the dockside. *Peter Rose*

BELOW: Trip 45 forming the local pick-up goods returning to Hull pulls into Hessle goods yard on 8th March 1958 hauled by J25 class 0-6-0 No. 65726.

ABOVE: Headed by Standard class 3 2-6-0 No. 77000 Trip 36 descends to Neptune Street on the H&B line from Springhead with empty mineral wagons. Notable in the right background are the flues of a fish curing factory where herrings were hung and smoked to turn them into kippers. There were many of these in the vicinity of the fish docks and two examples survive in 2016 near Hessle Road Junction. *D P. Leckonby*

BELOW: N10 0-6-2T No. 69093 rumbles Trip 104 from the eastern docks past Anlaby Road level crossing, years before it was replaced by a concrete flyover in 1964.

ABOVE: Trip 109 headed by K3 2-6-0 No. 61923 is on the Victoria Dock branch in this early 1950s view. It has been given the signal at Botanic Gardens to proceed off the line from Anlaby Road following the passage of a passenger train. *Tom Greaves*

BELOW: No. 118 trip hauled by K3 2-6-0 No. 61935 raises a few echoes as it passes Dairycoates West in energetic fashion on Tuesday 16th January 1962. Immediately behind the engine are two "Lowfit" wagons carrying Weekes' trailers. Trip 118 also served Melton cement works. *Peter Rose*

ABOVE: BELOW: The world stops while Trip 133 worked by B1 No. 61060, having ventured on to the Victoria Dock line, passes Botanic Gardens c1948 as it returns to Hull yards. The brake van of a goods train going the other way can just be seen. *Tom Greaves*

BELOW: With 133 trip returning fish vans from Paragon station, J94 0-6-0ST No. 68042 passes Hessle Road signal box on 18th January 1962. Modernisation work is under way and the footbridge has already been removed. During the course of the year, the mechanical signal box would be replaced by the power box that still controls the area in 2016. The H&B line from Springhead would be connected to the line shown, the section to Neptune Street abandoned and the girder bridge carrying it, from which the picture was taken, removed to make way for a road flyover in place of the level crossing, for which houses on the left have been demolished. *Peter Rose*

ABOVE: A trip working in the charge of WD 2-8-0 No. 90704 awaits clearance for the crossing while on its way out of Albert Dock to the exchange sidings on Friday 24th April 1964. The dock gates and gatehouse are straight ahead while a Scammel Scarab dray can just be seen between 90704's tender and the water column. *Peter Rose*

BELOW: No. 7 pilot at Albert Dock in November 1953 being worked by A7 4-6-2T No. 69773. No. 7 pilot worked from 5.20am until 9.20pm weekdays. It began with two return trips from Inward Yard to Manor House. Then, after the crew's breakfast, it worked from Belle Vue to Inward Yard and back to Manor House. After that it shunted at Old Creek, followed by weighbridge duties at Found Out Sidings and finally the 6.30pm from Manor House to Outward Yard. The remainder of the shift was undertaken according to the Dairycoates inspector's requirements.

ABOVE: On this day in June 1953, N10 0-6-2T No. 69093 was displaying a No. 9 pilot tablet at William Wright Dock. In the left background is the factory of British Ropes Ltd. Other factories in the area included engineering works and paint and varnish manufacturers - all industries which had grown to serve maritime requirements.

BELOW: J71 0-6-0T No. 68264 on No. 10 pilot at Albert Dock, 15th May 1959. No. 10 pilot worked 6am to 10pm weekdays as follows: "Shunts on Albert Dock. Works trips Inward Yard to Albert Dock, Albert Dock to Outward Yard and, as required, works coal and coal empties to and from Albert Dock. Then works for Dairycoates inspector shunting kit humps etc."

ABOVE: A policeman seems to have charge of movements at St. Andrew's Dock where J77 0-6-0T No. 68409 is on No. 22 pilot duty moving empty fish vans in June 1953. No. 22 pilot worked 6am Monday to 6am Saturday. Its instructions were: "Sets St. Andrew's Dock with fish empties. C&W 1pm. Shunts St. Andrews Dock until after departure of 5.30pm Doncaster fish. Marshalls trains at West End Outward Yard."

BELOW: Besides the big marshalling yards there were several groups of sidings dotted around Hull for sorting local traffic, such as those at Springhead, the riverside docks, the eastern docks and Southcoates. Pilot No. 25, by this time 204hp diesel shunter No. D2171, shunts Sweet Dews Sidings, Southcoates. Behind it, the Withernsea lines pass under the goods line coming down from the H&B at Bridges Junction to the joint line leading to King George Dock. Pilot 25 was one of eight Drypool pilots which shunted as required 6am to 10pm on weekdays. *Rev. David Benson*

ABOVE: Shunting No. 53 pilot at Alexandra Dock Junction is nearly new J72 0-6-0T No. 69011, built at Darlington c1950 and allocated to Alexandra Dock sub-shed. From here lines went right to the west side of the dock and timber storage yards, and left to the rest of the dock, Alexandra Dock sidings and King George Dock. Alexandra Dock signal box stands in the background.

BELOW: Hemmed in by ships and cranes, original J72 0-6-0T No. 68672 works No. 57 pilot shunting wagons loaded with timber on the quayside at Alexandra Dock in April 1949. Nos. 53 and 57 pilots were both booked to shunt Alexandra dock as required from 6am Monday to 6am Sunday, and were among eight pilots allocated to work there.

ABOVE: Stabled between duties at Alexandra Dock in the early days of British Railways are J77 0-6-0 tanks Nos. E8402 and 68401, the former wearing pilot No. 98 tablet which meant it was available to shunt at King George Dock if required. Alexandra Dock supplied nine pilots for King George Dock each day. This stabling point was classed as a sub-shed of Springhead depot and the Hull & Barnsley Railway had a timber engine shed here. Standing above the engines is the pumping station which provided hydraulic power for much of the dock machinery. In the right background is ex-Hull & Barnsley Railway sand van No. 1817.

BELOW: J94 Austerity 0-6-0ST No. 68042 shunts Hull Central goods depot on Wednesday 13th November 1963. Hull Central, situated between Manor House Road and Humber Dock, marked the end of the original 1840 line from Selby. *Peter Rose*

ABOVE: Eight pilots from Dairycoates shed that were required to shunt Victoria Dock, its timber yards and other yards in the area were out-stationed at Drypool. This view of Drypool stabling point during the lunchtime break on Wednesday 12th September 1956 shows, from left: J71 0-6-0T No. 68230, J72s 68753, 68718 and 68751, and J71 No. 68232.

BELOW: These short wheelbase Sentinel 4-wheel vertical boilered chain-drive locomotives were ideal for sharp curves such as those on to the docksides, and were used to shunt parts of Victoria Dock not accessible to the 0-6-0 tank engines, two being required each day. This view shows class Y1 No. 68148 there on 13th June 1954.

ABOVE: Huge volumes of imported timber came in through Victoria Dock and wagons can be seen here loaded with sawn planks. Tow motors - tractors equipped with buffing plates front and rear - were also used for shunting around the dock as seen on the right. On Sunday 13th June 1954 this class Y3 Sentinel loco was still displaying its LNER number, 8183, on the buffer beam.

BELOW: At Victoria Dock these wooden bogies seen on Thursday 12th January 1967 were used for moving sawn timber from ship to storage area. They had only the most rudimentary dumb buffers and couplings and were hauled by a tractor using a chain. Behind are old main line wagons relegated to internal use around the dock and for timber storage, being known as "No go greens" because they had "dock use only" stencilled on a green panel. The plate on the bogie reads: "LNER HO 7 TONS 09841 TIMBER BOGIE." The wagon behind is possibly of Midland Railway origin and has "DOCK USE ONLY 054729" stencilled on the green panel. *Peter Rose*

ABOVE: In 2016 only the two main running lines of the Hull-Scarborough route remain at Cottingham South but this scene on Thursday 10th September 1959 shows that there were once far more. Coming in from the right is the original Hull & Selby Bridlington branch from Hessle Road while on the left are sidings serving the Ideal Boilers and Radiators factory. They are being shunted by Ideal's 1947-built 0-4-0 Fowler diesel. Many private establishments around the city had their own shunting engines. Today there are none and Ideal was among the last of them.

BELOW: The point where it all came together, the sprawling marshalling yards in west Hull, all of which no longer exist, having been closed and redeveloped as a large trading estate. This view shows the Inward Yard where incoming wagons would descend by gravity from a hump into the various sidings according to their destinations in Hull. On the right is the North branch and beyond that the Priory Yard. In the left distance is the tower of Pickering Road church which had to be demolished on safety grounds.

Engine sheds. The railways of Hull and its docks were so extensive that they required three major locomotive depots to provide them with all the engines necessary to move the traffic they generated. Far and away the biggest of these was Dairycoates, in fact it was the biggest engine shed in the North East. It provided mainly goods and shunting engines as well as some passenger locomotives, especially in later years when it also became home to Hull's diesel locomotive fleet.

Botanic Gardens, conveniently situated for Paragon station, provided passenger engines. In the late 1950s it was completely rebuilt as a modern diesel depot for the many multiple units that were taking over most passenger services in the area, including the famous Trans-Pennine trains.

Springhead was the engine shed for the Hull & Barnsley and its job was to provide engines to cover all traffic on the lines originating with that company. Adjoining it was the H&B's locomotive works and carriage and wagon shops, while it also had a sub-shed at Alexandra Dock where shunting engines were outbased. After the H&B was absorbed into the NER in 1922 and then the LNER in 1923, Springhead steadily lost its importance and the locomotive works, especially, saw less and less work until it became little more than a store for spare or redundant engines. Springhead closed in December 1958 upon closure of the H&B as a through route but at the same time was adapted for use as a diesel depot until the rebuilding of Botanic Gardens had been fully completed.

Decline in docks traffic during the 1960s and a general reduction in railborne freight led to the unthinkable - the closure of Dairycoates in 1970. Its diesel shunters were transferred to Botanic Gardens while any main line locomotives required were brought from other depots, such as York and Tinsley, and stabled and refuelled at Botanic Gardens. Botanic Gardens has survived, caring for those diesel units that provide the remaining local services but is now very much slimmed down.

Shafts of sunlight illuminate WD 2-8-0s Nos. 90284, 90700 and 90378, K3 2-6-0 No. 61819 and, extreme right, J6 0-6-0 No. 64170, as they stand round one of Dairycoates' six roundhouse turntables. It also had a straight shed.

ABOVE: This is Dairycoates West Junction as seen from a passenger train to Selby on Wednesday 8th August 1962. It was also known as Murray Mint Junction because according to rumour one signalman would, when it got too busy, throw all the levers to stop, sit down and have a smoke, and thus would not hurry - as per the Murray Mints advert "too good to hurry mints." The huge engine shed, as rebuilt in the 1950s, fills the background left of the signal box. On the far left stands its mammoth coaling plant - the "cracker" - which when built in the early 1900s was one of the first to be powered by electricity. The lines to the riverside docks and Manor House are right of the signal box. The engine shed still stands in 2016, in private use as a warehouse.

BELOW: As well as coal, steam engines need water - lots of it and it has to be soft water otherwise the limescale will soon ruin the boiler tubes. With its chalk wolds, East Yorkshire is an area of very hard water and so this huge water softening plant situated at Hessle was needed. A withdrawn former NER class C6 Atlantic locomotive No. 2939 can be seen in use as a stationary boiler. June 1947.

ABOVE: An array of classic NER goods tank engines inside Dairycoates shed on Sunday 18th May 1952. From left, they are: N8 0-6-2 No. 69385, a class dating back to 1886, N10 0-6-2 No. 69106, A7 Pacifics Nos. 69788 and 69782, and N8 No. 69377. It is interesting to note that 69377 has lining on the tank sides denoting a mixed traffic or passenger locomotive, as some N8s were, but this one appears not to be equipped with vacuum brake for working passenger trains.

BELOW: And out in the open on Sunday 11th October 1959 after one of the roundhouses had been demolished. Engines on view are, from left: J71 0-6-0 tank No. 68264, a class dating from 1886, J72 0-6-0T No. 69003, a class dating from 1898 but this one from a batch built by British Railways at Darlington in the early 1950s, and on the right, J73 0-6-0T No. 68363. In the middle is J39 0-6-0 tender engine No. 64914. These mixed traffic engines, designed by Sir Nigel Gresley, were introduced in 1926 and were one of the many steam types to be rendered extinct at a stroke in December 1962.

ABOVE: The coal plant was taken out of use before Dairycoates shed actually closed to steam in June 1967 and the conveyor seen in this picture was used for coaling the few remaining steam locomotives. A handful of WD 2-8-0s and a couple of B1 4-6-0s continued to work local trips until the Paxman diesels arrived from the Western Region, this WD in April 1967 being No. 90670. *Peter Rose*

BELOW: Botanic Gardens engine shed on Sunday 18th May 1952 when still a steam shed. On the left is the old coal stage which had been replaced in 1932 by a mechanical coaling plant out of view behind the water tower. A roundhouse with two internal turntables, the shed was opened in 1901 to replace older engine sheds at Paragon which were demolished to make room for expansion of the station. Botanic Gardens closed to steam in June 1959 and was rebuilt as a modern diesel depot. It is still in use today but unrecognisable from this view.

ABOVE: The D49 "Shire" and "Hunt" 4-4-0s, designed by Sir Nigel Gresley and introduced by the LNER in 1927 were staple power for many passenger services from Hull until the arrival of diesels. In the early days of British Railways, "Shire" No. 62724 *Bedfordshire* is refilled with water while "Hunt" No. 62754 *The Berkeley* makes use of the manually operated outdoor turntable. In those days, hard, physical graft was a normal part of everyday life. In 1950 no less than 13 D49s were allocated to Botanic Gardens. *Tom Greaves*

BELOW: Also staple power for passenger services until the advent of diesels were the older ex-NER D20 4-4-0s, although few were allocated to Hull. Nos. 62396 and 62381 had been in store out of use at Dairycoates but it was decided to use them once more to help with heavy summer traffic in 1957. But someone in authority thought they looked much too scruffy to be seen in service so they sent for a painter from Darlington who smartened them up complete with the new BR totem on their tenders. The pair are seen behind the old coal stage at Botanic Gardens depot on Friday 13th September 1957 following conclusion of the summer timetable and awaiting transfer to Alnmouth in Northumberland where, alas, they were soon withdrawn from service.

ABOVE: As an economy measure, the LNER introduced steam-powered railcars to some branch line services in the 1920s. Built by Sentinel of Shrewsbury and based on that manufacturer's steam lorry, they were named after old stagecoaches and most continued in service until the late 1940s. Among services in the Hull area operated by Sentinel railcars were those over the H&B to South Howden. Pictured here is *Highflyer* with another Sentinel at Botanic Gardens depot on Wednesday 9th August 1939.

BELOW: Diesels first came to Botanic Gardens as along ago as the early 1930s but steam would then reign for another 25 years. *Lady Hamilton,* seen here at Botanic depot in August 1939, was one of three diesel electric prototypes produced on Tyneside by Armstrong Whitworth in 1931 and taken into LNER service. She was the last of the three to remain in operation.

ABOVE: The main erecting shop at Springhead locomotive works in LNER days when still used for repair work. On the right is NER class M 4-4-0 No. 1637(LNER class D17/1) while in the centre is Robinson Great Central design 2-8-0 No. 6632, LNER class O4. The LNER transferred a number of these engines to the H&B to replace older H&B 0-8-0s.

BELOW: In the Springhead erecting shop during in the late 1940s is ex-NER J77 0-6-0T No. 8429, soon to become BR No. 68429. On the left is a WD 2-8-0 while the engine parted from its tender in the background is D49 4-4-0 No. 2722 *Huntingdonshire*. Springhead was equipped to undertake the heaviest repairs but its workload declined steadily after the H&B was absorbed by the NER.

ABOVE: Springhead lacked the convenience of a mechanical coal hopper and engines were coaled using tubs loaded by hand and then tipped from the ramped coal stage. In 1949 J25 0-6-0 No. 65654 has its tender filled simultaneously with coal and water.

BELOW: The H&B class F3 0-6-2 tanks which became LNER class N13 were the last H&B engines to remain in service and ten examples even made it into the British Railways era. This is No. 69111 at Springhead on Sunday 30th July 1950.

ABOVE: H&B class G3 0-6-0 tank(LNER class J75) No. 2524 on pilot duty at Springhead c1936. Rebuilt from their original domeless boiler form in the 1920s, this was the only one making it into BR service, as No. 68365, but it was withdrawn in 1949.

BELOW: An oft-seen view but who can resist it! It is such a wonderful example of two of Hull's transport forms coming together in one scene. With two ships in the Graving Dock, eleven class J72 0-6-0 tanks rest at the Alexandra Dock "sub-shed" in April 1954. There was once a wooden engine shed here but by 1927 it had become so dilapidated that it had to be demolished. The overall scene today is unrecognisable except that the dry dock is still used by a ship repair company.

Alien visitors. Hull may have been at the far end of the line but it wasn't too isolated to be visited by foreign engines from company origins alien to its already rich variety of North Eastern, Hull & Barnsley and LNER types. In fact, from opening up of the direct route to Doncaster via Goole in 1869 the Lancashire & Yorkshire and Manchester, Sheffield & Lincolnshire Railways had running powers to Hull. In the BR era, some locomotive types of London Midland & Scottish Railway origin were allocated to Hull sheds

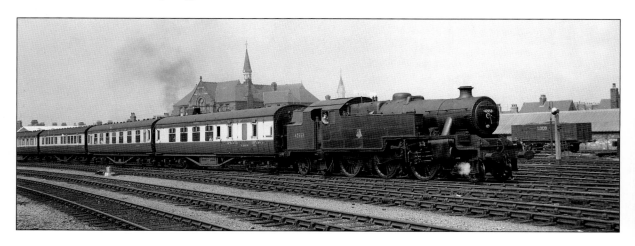

ABOVE: Heading a truly smart rake of coaches in BR crimson and cream - otherwise known as "blood and custard" - Goole-based Stanier 2-6-4 tank No. 42553 approaches Paragon station in the 1950s with the daily express from Wakefield via Goole, a former Lancashire & Yorkshire Railway service.

Two tank engines were regularly used on this service, 42553 and 42477 and it was always a laugh to see the number of times local spotters would write down 62477 *Glen Dochart*. On one occasion, this train failed to stop at Paragon and smashed into some wooden buildings that stood across the concourse end of the platforms. They contained a barber's shop and it was amazing how five men all managed to get through its narrow door at the same time!

BELOW: This strange contraption visiting Springhead depot is a Great Western Railway "Dean Goods" 0-6-0 with added pannier tanks and condensing apparatus while in War Department service as WD No. 199. Its reason for being in Hull has been lost in the mists of time but it was one of a pair that were seeing war service in Lincolnshire at the time.

ABOVE: This visitor seen at Cottingham South on Thursday 10th September 1959 is ex-Lancashire & Yorkshire Railway Aspinall 2F 0-6-0 No. 52319 doing the rounds with water cans for signal boxes, a number of which had no mains water supply. These and other ex-L&Y engines were never too far away from Hull, being in their normal habitat at Goole which is where 52319 was normally based. However, it had a short spell at Selby and then at Hull during which time it saw use on trains clearing fallen chalk from the steep cutting at Kirkella on the H&B line.

BELOW: Among various ex-LMS engines allocated to Hull for a time in the early 1960s were 3F 0-6-0 tanks. No. 47632 passes Hessle Road level crossing while going to Chalk Lane sidings to work 22B pilot duty on Tuesday 28th June 1960. Dairycoates was custodian of 47632 and three others in 1960/61.

ABOVE: Among the more unusual engines to find themselves in Hull following nationalisation were these ex-LMS Fowler class 3P 2-6-2 tanks. No less than eight of these aliens were allocated to Botanic Gardens but few were the men who had a good word for them and they spent much of their time at Hull in store. No. 40061, however, has found work as Paragon station pilot. On the smokebox door it is still wearing the 26F code of its former home depot which was Lees, Oldham.

BELOW: Class C12 Atlantic tank No. 67395 adds Great Northern Railway flavour to the mix while bringing empty coaches into Paragon station on Friday 29th August 1952. Back in the early 1950s they would not be so foreign as eight were allocated to Botanic Gardens for local passenger and empty stock duties. They also bear a family resemblance to the Hull & Barnsley engines. Hardly surprising as H&B engines were designed by Matthew Stirling, son of the GNR locomotive engineer Patrick Stirling, although the C12s themselves were designed by his successor H. A. Ivatt.

ABOVE: This Great Northern visitor simmering inside Dairycoates shed in 1956 is Bradford-based J6 0-6-0 No. 64226. It had arrived with an overnight goods from Keighley that was often referred to as "The Wringer." During the day, the engine off this train would often be put to work on the Beverley or Bridlington trip before returning home the next night.

BELOW: Enthusiasts' railtours could usually be relied upon to bring unusual locomotives to any town or city and Hull was no exception. Having reached Hull via the H&B line, this special for the Railway Correspondence & Travel Society brought a Great Eastern engine in the form of Lincoln-based D16 4-4-0 No. 62571. It is seen in the exchange sidings at Albert Dock.

A FOREIGNER RECALLED

We had a B12 turn up in Hull on 14th May 1959. The Institution of Water Engineers had a meeting in Lincoln and wanted to visit a new reservoir being built near Driffield. At first they intended to use the ferry and hire some buses but then one of their number by the name of Walter Skeet, decided they should have a train. They organised a five-coach special and the Eastern Region offered them a choice of engine. They asked for a B12. There weren't many left by then but 61577 was found at Cambridge, sent up to Lincoln, bulled up and put on the train which went to Driffield via Market Weighton.

After Driffield it had to go to Bridlington to service the coaches and turn the engine. But the engine was found to have a hot axlebox on one of the driving wheels and so had to be sent at slow speed to Dairycoates for repairs, its replacement, by coincidence, being B1 No.

The beautiful B12 4-6-0s originated on the Great Eastern Railway to the design of J. Holden; most were rebuilt as B12/3 in the 1930s to the design of Sir Nigel Gresley. B12/3 No. 61577 is pictured on the site of Dairycoates No. 3 shed on 20th May 1959 after having had its overheating axlebox repaired.

In fact the B12s were regular pre-war visitors to Hull with the 10.5am express from York via Market Weighton(as with original B12 No. 1561E pictured in Railway Memories No. 1 York, Bellcode Books 1988,) returning to Doncaster with an afternoon fish train.

61377. Meanwhile, 61577 was put on the wheel drop to get the wheels off and repair the box.

Of course, I knew nothing of all this. This was on the Thursday. By chance, on the Saturday 16th May I went on my scooter over the ferry and down to Cambridge shed. There, the foreman asked: "Where's our B12? We sent a B12 up to you and it hasn't come back."

When I got home I rang Dairycoates and asked: "Have you by any chance got 61577?"

"Yes, it's in the wheeldrop." came the reply.

Within half an hour I was down there and got photos of it on the drops and later in steam on the shed. Eventually it worked 32 pilot to Melton, just to run it in. I went to Hessle and asked the signalman to stop it for a moment so that I could get a shot. I was on the opposite platform, four roads over. So I got my photo and then dived across the tracks and into the brake van. The startled guard looked at me and said "Who the *!∂*! are you?"

I said: "I'm coming with you to Melton."

"OK," he said, "But keep out of sight."

We got to Melton and my pal Peter Harrod turned up on his BSA motor bike. We took more pictures and then he brought me back to Hessle.

ON THE WATER. *Maybe it's a case of saving the most important till last because without the water and the ships, boats, barges and ferries that sail upon it, Kingston-upon-Hull would not be the port and city that it is.*

Among the plethora of cargos handled by Hull came wool from Australia, butter and lamb from New Zealand, cocoa beans from Africa, bacon from Denmark, oil for the refinery at Saltend, endless stacks of timber from Scandinavia and, of course there was the fish. And whether it was machine tools and carpets from Halifax, tractors from Huddersfield or coal from Barnsley, it all went out through Hull. These were times when Britain manufactured for the world. So busy and packed with ships were the docks that not all incoming vessels could find an immediate berth and had to wait at anchor in the estuary. If they had perishable cargo on board barges known as lighters would be used to ferry it ashore.

Victoria Dock is now gone. Alexandra Dock closed to commercial shipping in 1983 after two decades of decline at the port, but was reopened in 1993 and is now host to a giant wind turbine factory. An extension to King George Dock fpr handling containers opened in 1969 and was named Queen Elizabeth Dock. Today the two handle the bulk of the shipping, from cargo vessels, container ships and bulk carriers to continental ferries and even cruise liners. The docks in the west have enjoyed a revival also.

Looking at Humber Dock today, reduced to a marina devoted mainly to pleasure boats - along with Railway Dock - it is incredible to think that not so long ago this was where the ferries and cargo ships set sail for the near continent - almost from the city centre in fact. Hull-Rotterdam sailings were operated by Associated Humber Lines, a joint enterprise involving British Railways, the Hull & Netherlands Steam Ship Co. Ltd., and Wilson's & North Eastern Railway Shipping Co. Ltd.(Wilson's being Ellerman's Wilson Line, until 1916 the Wilson Line - a great Hull shipping line founded in 1825 and which had a steamship sailing between Hull and Gothenberg as early as 1840.) In summer 1957, for example, the S.S. Melrose Abbey and S.S. Bury shared sailings from Hull on Wednesdays and Saturdays and from Rotterdam on Tuesdays and Saturdays. Ellerman's Wilson Line cargo steamers between Hull and Antwerp and Hull and Bremen could also carry passengers.

An 1870s plan to build a direct railway between North Lincolnshire and Hull via a tunnel under the Humber failed to complete its course through Parliament, not least because it was considered over ambitious in engineering terms. Consequently, ferries ruled the Humber crossing until completion of the Humber Bridge in 1981 when it was the world's longest suspension bridge. Of course, many estuaries have, or have had, ferries - the Mersey, the Thames, the Tyne, the Itchen - but the Humber ferries stood out because they were paddle steamers into the 1970s. The use of paddle steamers on the Humber goes back to 1832 with a vessel called the Magna Charta. In 1845 it was purchased by the Great Grimsby & Sheffield Junction Railway and over time the ferry service passed to the Great Central Railway, the LNER and finally British Rail. At one time the ferries continued along the Trent as far into Lincolnshire as Gainsborough. The final three "paddlers" were built in 1934 and 1940 as part of a general efficiency upgrade enabling motor vehicles to drive on and off whereas they had to be hoisted on and off the previous vessels by crane.

A page from the British Railways North Eastern Region summer 1950 timetable providing details of Associated Humber Lines sailings between Hull and the Continent.

ABOVE: The *S.S. Melrose Abbey 11* of Associated Humber Lines in Humber Dock while preparing for her final voyage to Rotterdam in 1959. Built for the Hull & Netherlands Steamship Co. in 1929 at Earle's shipyard in Hull, she served as a convoy rescue ship in world war two, making 14 life-saving voyages. She had been renamed from just *Melrose Abbey* in 1958 so that a new diesel vessel could carry the Melrose Abbey name. She was then sold to a Greek line and worked until 1966, finally being broken up in 1980. The *MV Melrose Abbey* sailed the Hull-Rotterdam route until Associated Humber Lines was disbanded in 1971.

BELOW: The *S.S. Holdernain,* seen in Humber Dock on Sunday 17th May 1959, had a long and distinguished history. Built in 1923 as a coal-fired triple expansion steamship named *Frank*, she was originally part of the Norwegian merchant fleet. In 1932 she was sold to new Scandinavian owners and renamed *Skarv.* In 1943 she arrived in Scotland and was deployed on British coastal convoy duty but her finest hour came when she made several voyages to Omaha Beach in support of the D. Day landings. She was converted to oil firing in 1952 and the next year was sold to the Holderness Steamship Co. when she was named *Holdernain.* Established in 1945, the Holderness Steamship Co. specialized in buying up old steamers, applying new names starting with "Holdern" and operating them around the coast and to the near Continent until they became uneconomic. Cozrelwaves Ltd. bought *Holdernain* in 1963 and renamed her *Emmanuella* but she was laid up in Trieste, Italy, that same year and broken up there.

ABOVE: The *S. S. Hebble* was built on the Clyde by Beardmores shipyard in 1924, the first of four sisters for the Goole-Antwerp service, but she is seen here embarking from Humber Dock on Wednesday 25th March 1959. Her name gives away her Lancashire & Yorkshire Railway origin, the Hebble being a tributary of the River Calder along whose valley in West Yorkshire the L&Y main line passes. She was withdrawn in 1959.

BELOW: The *S.S. Bury* enters Humber Dock from the estuary on Monday 18th May 1959. The *Bury* was built for the Great Central Railway by Earles in 1911. She was trapped in Hamburg when war broke out in 1914 and the crew were taken prisoner, a stewardess later being released following representations by the United States. More trouble in Germany followed in 1936 when she collided on the River Elbe with a German steamer which sank, *Bury's* crew rescuing the German crew. She also served as a convoy rescue ship in world war 11 and was scrapped in 1958.

ABOVE: The diesel ship *MV Fountains Abbey* at Humber Dock on Sunday 17th May 1959 with a railway goods container on the deck. Built in 1954 by Hall, Russell & Co. of Aberdeen, she caught fire in 1962 while on a passage from Bremen. She was towed back to Ijmuiden and declared a total loss. The AHL Hull-Rotterdam service ceased in 1971 following a steady decline in traditional passenger and cargo traffic. Nowadays, huge vessels up to 60,000 tonnes operated by North Sea Ferries - an amalgam of P&O and Dutch interests - provide roll-on roll-off services for cars and lorries as well as passengers between King George Dock, Rotterdam and Zeebrugge.

BELOW: Cargo being unloaded from *The Hebble* in Humber Dock on Wednesday 25th March 1959. *Melrose Abbey 11* is alongside.

ABOVE: A somewhat inactive Riverside Quay with Norwegian freighter *Torpo* at anchor in 1972, as seen from the Humber ferry. Ferries to the continent once sailed from here served directly by boat trains under the auspices of both the North Eastern and Lancashire & Yorkshire railways. Boat trains ceased using Riverside quay in 1938 and it was destroyed by bombing in the blitz of May 1941. The quay was rebuilt and reopened in 1959 but without the boat trains. In 1965 North Sea Ferries was formed using much larger vessels sailing from the eastern docks, setting the stage for today's ferry operations. *Stephen Chapman*

BELOW: A vital aspect of port business are the various support vessels such as pilots and tugs and their highly skilled crews whose job it is to ensure the safe passage of all ships. No less than five tugs, for estuary and river use, are seen moored in Railway Dock on Wednesday 25th September 1963. They are the *Pinky, Waterman, Boatman, Marksman and Tradesman*. *Peter Rose*

ABOVE: In this early 1950s view, tug *Cockspur* turns the freighter *Milford Duchess* ready for her departure from Prince's Dock.
Tom Greaves

BELOW: Most of the seemingly endless trainloads of coal coming into Hull ended up at the docks where the black stuff was loaded into ships. This is one of the coal hoists at Alexandra Dock during the loading of a collier, possibly some time in the early 1950s. A railway wagon can be seen through the girders being tipped so that the coal will run out and down the chute. *Picture by courtesy of ABP*

ABOVE: The biggest dock and the one primarily used today is King George Dock, opened in 1914 as a joint venture by the North Eastern and Hull & Barnsley railways. This busy view looking east dates from the 1930s and shows large ships as far as the eye can see as well as an array of tugs and lighters. Over on the left are extensive railway sidings and beyond them open countryside.
Mike Thompson collection

RIGHT: The west end of King George Dock in the late 1960s following construction of the roll-on roll-off ferry berth.
The sidings are less busy than in the previous view, reflecting a decline in railborne traffic, but there are still plenty of lighters present.
Picture by courtesy of ABP

ABOVE: This undated postcard view shows Alexandra Dock packed with ships including the *Saturnus* in the foreground. Alexandra Dock was established by the Hull & Barnsley Railway and Dock Co. in 1885, closed 98 years later and then subsequently reopened without its once extensive railway. *Courtesy R. Woodmore*

BELOW: Docks and channels had to be kept to the required depth in order to safely accommodate the ships that needed to use them and with the Humber's shifting sand banks it was a full time job for the dredgers. This is the Hull & Barnsley Railway's steam dredger *Precursor* which would have been used to keep the eastern docks clear.

ABOVE: St. Andrew's Dock was home to Hull's great North Sea fishing fleet until the industry was almost wiped out in the 1970s by the loss of key fishing grounds through Common Market(now the European Union) restrictions imposed on Britain in the wake of the Cod War, an armed dispute at sea between Britain and Iceland over fishing rights. Today the dock is completely silted up and returned to nature but there are proposals to reinstate it as a heritage dock. *Malcolm Fussey*

BELOW: At the west end of St. Andrew's Dock was St. Andrew's Dock Extension and at the end of that was a slipway where boats were hauled up for repairs. This 1930s view shows three steam fishing boats undergoing hull repairs and painting with the *Welsbach* on the left and the *James Barrie* centre. Railway vans can be seen in the Outward Yard on the right. *Harry Cartlidge*

ABOVE: In this 1950s scene, Sunday sight-seers gather on the St. Andrew's Dock landing stage for the arrival of the steam trawler *Victrix* upon her return from the fishing grounds. Women can be seen on the landing stage but it was considered bad luck for them to be on St. Andrew's Dock itself. In the far distance is the Riverside Quay clocktower, the only part of Riverside Quay to survive the 1941 blitz. *Mike Thompson collection*

BELOW: Humber Dock looking towards the city on Wednesday 25th September 1963. On the right, a lorry crosses the bridge over the entrance to Prince's Dock while the wooden coble, *Johanna* is the nearest vessel. *Peter Rose*

ABOVE: The Spurn light ship was an important navigation aid to ships entering and leaving the Humber estuary which can be even more treacherous than usual at night. She is seen here in Albert Dock on Tuesday 23rd June 1964. She is now preserved and permanently moored in the Humber Dock marina. *Peter Rose*

BELOW: Besides passenger ferries, the Great Central Railway operated a goods ferry using lighters between New Holland Creek and Hull Creek - also variously known as "Railway Wharf," "Railway Creek," "Old Creek" or "Old Wharf." This picture of New Holland Creek is undated but was taken in the 1920s or early 1930s with LNER-owned lighters and, in the distance, a pair of earlier generation paddle steamers at the pier. It can also just be seen that the pier station had an overall trainshed roof.

LEFT: The new Drypool Bridge is raised for the passage of two barges including the sail barge *Thyras* along the River Hull while on their way out into the Humber on Tuesday 31st October 1961. Barges like this were once a familiar sight on the waterways feeding into the Humber but are now just a part of the area's fascinating transport history.

The picture is taken from just by the Rank flour mills in the old harbour area where the first quay was built in 1293 for King Edward 1's navy during his campaigns against the Scots. As a result, what was then the town of Wyke-on-Hull was granted King's town status and renamed Kingston-upon-Hull. The river Hull entrance to Victoria Dock is behind the photographer while North Bridge can be seen in the distance. Behind the old warehouses lining the opposite bank of the river is High Street and the old town. *Peter Rose*

BELOW: This view of the River Hull is from the Wilmington swing bridge carrying the railway to Victoria Dock, Hornsea and Withernsea. Flanked by riverside wharves, barges go about their trade while a larger vessel can just be seen behind the crane on the right. *Rev. David Benson*

ABOVE: In order that this section on the Humber's wonderful paddle steamers doesn't end on a sorry note this picture is dealt with first. The view is William Wright Dock during the 1970s and paddler *Lincoln Castle* is looking very woebegone alongside the Globe boiler works. It may be 1978 and she has been withdrawn after failing a boiler inspection. She carries the British Rail(Sealink) logo on her funnel while berthed beyond her is a small collection of trawlers.

BELOW: Spectacular the Humber Bridge may be, but crossing it by car or bus just doesn't have the same magic as setting sail for Lincolnshire by paddle steamer. On Sunday 17th May 1959, one of the Humber's three paddle steamers, *Wingfield Castle,* arrives at Victoria Pier, as the floating jetty at Corporation Pier was properly known. *Wingfield Castle* was built in Hartlepool in 1934 and is now moored there as a floating restaurant.

TOP: A photograph taken from the railway inspector's office at Albert Dock on Thursday 7th March 1963 as paddle steamers pass. *Peter Rose*

CENTRE: Famous as the railway station which never had any trains - and, as it happens, a station originally belonging to a "foreign" railway so far as Hull was concerned - the Great Central Railway. This is Corporation Pier station in February 1997 when offered for sale. It had waiting rooms, a ticket office, a parcels office and ferry offices on the first floor. As the stones on each side of the clock state, it was built in 1880 when the GC was still the Manchester, Sheffield & Lincolnshire Railway. The station closed in 1981 upon opening of the Humber Bridge. *Stephen Chapman*

BELOW: Seen from a ferry passing the other way, the *Lincoln Castle* leaves the Hull waterfront behind and makes for New Holland. Built in 1940, *Lincoln Castle* was by 1974 the only one of the three still in operation when she was the last coal-fired paddle steamer in daily public service. To help keep a decent level of service going, diesel electric paddler *Farringford* was transferred from the Isle of Wight and she worked a reduced service alone after *Lincoln Castle* was withdrawn in 1978. *Lincoln Castle* is the only one not with us today. After finding a new lease of life as a floating restaurant in Grimsby, she was scrapped in 2010.

ABOVE: Before she became a restaurant in Grimsby, *Lincoln Castle* was beached on the foreshore at Hessle, immediately below the new suspension bridge which had rendered the ferries redundant. She is seen here in 1982 with East Yorkshire Bristol VRT No. 519 for company.

BELOW: With the skyline of Hull ranged across the background, *Tattershall Castle*, built 1934, comes alongside the pier at New Holland on 12th May 1953. Happily, she is today a successful London bar and restaurant, moored on the Thames opposite the London Eye. In 2014 she came back to Hull for a complete refit and to have her hull strengthened.

Stepping off the ferry at New Holland was like entering another world. This was Lincolnshire, a very different county to Yorkshire and a place where the railways looked altogether different. North of the Humber was the North Eastern Region of British Railways where all the signs and station nameboards were tangerine; this was the Eastern Region where they were dark blue while the railway's heritage hereabouts was mainly from the Manchester, Sheffield & Lincolnshire Railway - the Great Central Railway from 1899. The Great Central had opened Immingham Dock in 1912 and it ran all the railway at New Holland, ferries included.

Once off the ferry, most passengers joined the next train for Grimsby and Cleethorpes and indeed what better day out could there be than a trip across the estuary on a paddle steamer, then a steam train to the delights of the seaside at Cleethorpes.

ABOVE: Ex-Great Northern Railway K2 2-6-0 No. 61727 awaits departure from New Holland Pier on 12th May 1953. To the left is an ex-Great Central J11 0-6-0.

BELOW: Another K2, this one No. 61745, propels empty coaches towards New Holland Pier on bank holiday Sunday 2nd August 1959, ready for the 10.20am non-stop additional train to Cleethorpes.

Railway Memories titles from BELLCODE BOOKS

Titles currently available, with recommended retail price:

No.9 WARRINGTON 122 photos. 72 pages. ISBN 9781871233 08 7. £9.50

No.14 SELBY & GOOLE Over 190 photos. 112 pages. ISBN 9781871233 14 8. £12.95

No.15 PONTEFRACT, CASTLEFORD & KNOTTINGLEY Over 190 photos. 112 pages. ISBN 9781871233 15 5. £12.95

No. 19 YORK TO SCARBOROUGH, WHITBY & RYEDALE 194 photos. 112 pages. ISBN9781871233 19 3. £13.95

No. 22 RETURN TO LEEDS 217 photos 112 pages. ISBN 9781871233 22 3 £13.95

No. 23 NORTHALLERTON, RIPON & WENSLEYDALE 184 photos. 112 pages. ISBN 9781871233 23 0. £13.95

No. 24 HARROGATE & WETHERBY 174 photos. 112 pages. ISBN 9781871233 24 7 £14.99

No. 25 STEAM AGE DIESELS ACROSS YORKSHIRE 188 photos 96 pages ISBN 9781871233 25 4 £13.99

No.26 THE TRIALS AND THE TRIUMPH A BR motive power professional's experience of the steam-diesel transition years. By Tom Greaves. 168 photos 112 pages ISBN 9781871233 26 1 £14.99

No.27 SHEFFIELD 220 photos 128 pages. ISBN 9781871233 28 5 £16.99

No.28 TYNESIDE and the Tyne Valley line 230 photos 128 pages ISBN9781871233 29 2 £17.99

No.29 THE BLYTH & TYNE *and associated colliery railways* 196 photos 112 pages ISBN9781871233 31 5. £15.99

More titles from Bellcode Books...........

KINGSTON-UPON-HULL. Images of a Rich Transport Heritage. 205 black and white photos of trains, trams, buses, trolley buses and shipping during their heyday. ISBN 9781871233 30 8. 112 pages £15.99

PICTORIAL DIARY No.1 LAST TRAIN TO HAULAGE HEAVEN.
Diesel hauled passenger trains since 1971. 129 colour photos. ISBN 9781871233 27 8 128 pages £14.99

Out of print titles no longer available from the publisher: Railway Memories No.1 York; Nos. 2 and 17 Darlington & South West Durham; No.3 Leeds; No.4 Bradford: No.5 Return to York; No.6 Ardsley, Wakefield & Normanton; No.7 Airedale & Wharfedale; No.8 Barnsley, Cudworth & Royston; No.10 Doncaster; No.11 Halifax & the Calder Valley; No.12 The Hull & Barnsley Railway; No.13 Huddersfield, Dewsbury & Batley; No. 16 West Riding Steam 1955-1969; No.18 Cleveland & Whitby; No. 20 West Riding Steam Pictorial; No.21 Rotherham, Mexborough & Wath; Fearless Ghosts. Second hand, specialist dealers and online sources may be able to help or you might find them still in the retail supply chain or on ebay. **Bellcode titles can be ordered** direct from Bellcode Books, Church View, Middle Street, Rudston, East Yorkshire YO25 4UF. Email bellcode4books@yahoo.co.uk for further information. Our titles can also be bought or ordered from bookshops, online booksellers and ebay.

In 2017, the year that Kingston-upon-Hull is Britain's City of Culture, it is most appropriate that the work of the archivist photographer should celebrate the diverse forms of transport that served this East Yorkshire port throughout the 20th century.

This collection of photographs is not intended to be an in depth study of Hull's railways, shipping or buses but more a nostalgic look back at what for many of us was a more interesting and inspiring era.

It recalls a time when the streets were dominated by push-bikes, mopeds, buses, trams and trolley buses, a time when steam ruled the rails and the waves. A time before the bridge and when Lincolnshire seemed like a foreign land.

£15.99

9 781871 233308 >

Bellcode
Books

KEY TO

Writing

BOOK **3**

CHRISTINE MOORCROFT ◆ LES RAY